FAMILY RIGHTS
Family Law and Medical Advance

This collection is for J. K. Mason, Professor Emeritus of Forensic Medicine in the University of Edinburgh. His unparalleled contribution to medico-legal studies may be monument enough, but here is further tribute

FAMILY RIGHTS
Family Law and Medical Advance

edited by
Elaine Sutherland
and
Alexander McCall Smith

EDINBURGH UNIVERSITY PRESS

© Edinburgh University Press 1990
22 George Square, Edinburgh

Distributed in North America
by Columbia University Press,
New York

Set in Alphacomp Goudy
by Pioneer Associates, Perthshire, and
printed in Great Britain by
The Alden Press Ltd, Oxford

British Library Cataloguing
 in Publication Data
Family rights.
1. Medicine. Legal aspects 2. Medicine.
 Ethical aspects
I. McCall Smith, Alexander 1948–
II. Sutherland, Elaine
342.441

ISBN 0 7486 0204 6

Introduction: The changing family

There must be very few people who can be indifferent to changes in family patterns. Social theorists, criminologists, politicians, economists, and demographers have all remarked on the way in which changes in patterns of family formation and family life have affected the functioning of society. The nature of the change itself differs in kind and degree from society to society, but what can be observed is a general move from the extended family, by way of the classical mother/father/children unit, to the widely-accepted options of the single parent family or the informal, extra-marital partnership.

The factors behind these changes are diverse, and most of them have been subjected to extensive study. We understand therefore the impact of urbanization and of the effect of the increased absorption of women into the workplace. We know of the effect of changing attitudes towards marriage itself and of the consequences that this has for the rapidly disappearing concept of illegitimacy. And we are familiar, too, with the economic and psychological sequelae of heightened divorce rates. All of these changes, of course, have had a considerable impact on family law, which has over recent decades been one of the most rapidly-developing areas of law.

This book is concerned with a particular set of influences on the family and with the implications of these changes for family law. These influences all result either from developments in the attitude of doctors and patients to medical treatment, or from scientific advances in medicine, particularly in the area of human reproduction. One question runs through all the chapters: how has family law responded to the fact that modern medicine has wrought significant changes in the relationship between parent and child, and between society and the family unit (whatever form the latter may take)?

Undoubtedly the most profound of the changes discussed here are those which affect the circumstances of human reproduction. These range from surrogacy (with or without medical involvement) to highly technical forms of extra-corporeal fertilization and embryo transfer. Two distinct sorts of question arise from these developments – how should they be regulated and what is the nature of the legal relationships to which they give rise? In the following chapters, these problems are addressed in particular by Bernard Dickens and Sheila McLean. Bernard Dickens points out just how dramatically the new technology affects traditional notions of the family, and just how severely what he sees as outdated legal and social ideas will be tested by these developments. Both he and Sheila McLean detect in opponents of the new techniques an unsympathetic and outdated attitude towards women; an attitude which they feel should be combatted through facilitative court decisions and legislation. Some legislators and jurists have responded positively to this challenge; others appear to have felt threatened by what has been seen as a frontal assault on the traditional notions of genetic relationship and family bonds.

The implications of scientific advance are also of concern to Ian Pullen, a psychiatrist with a strong interest in the implications of genetic knowledge. The importance of consent and the patient's right to information has been extensively discussed in modern medico-legal writing, but in their enthusiastic espousal of the 'right to know', lawyers frequently ignore the psychological devastation which certain forms of information may cause. Ian Pullen's concern here is to demonstrate how information about genetic defects—particularly information about Huntingdon's Disease—can affect entire families, and how this information is therefore a family matter. From the legal point of view, this gives rise to important questions of confidentiality.

The other main concern of this book arises in a scientifically more prosaic context but also entails important family issues. David Meyers examines how certain medical decisions are inevitably family ones, concentrating on those at the beginning and the end of life. His analysis of American cases is of particular interest to the non-American lawyer, as courts in the United States have been much readier to involve themselves in matters which on this side of the Atlantic might never get a legal airing. Whether this has always been a good thing is another matter; but it must be said of the American system that it has led to a great deal of principled and dispassionate analysis of the acute moral problems that arise in the special care nursery or the intensive care ward.

The emphasis on family decision-making in life and death matters, endorsed by the American courts and accepted in practice in British medicine, does not appear in relation to decisions about the medical treatment of minors. Here the impact of the 'break-down' of the family is most evident. Since the decision of the House of Lords in the landmark *Gillick* case,[1] analyzed here by Douglas Cusine, the

Introduction: The changing family

right of minors to seek contraceptive treatment without parental consent has been given judicial recognition in England (Scotland's position involves different legal issues). Parental involvement is thereby, for the majority of cases, no longer necessary. Similarly, a handful of decisions relating to the non-treatment of handicapped infants point to the limited significance of parental rights, rights which in the medico-legal context are beginning to look remarkably threadbare. In his discussion of the nature of parental rights in relation to the medical treatment of children, Alexander McCall Smith concludes that such rights must now be regarded as almost completely subservient to society's right to protect the welfare of the child. Few medical decisions are therefore going to be a matter of complete discretion for the parent, a conclusion which further underlines that the modern family reflects the individualistic spirit of the age.

Elaine Sutherland explores this theme further, questioning the legitimacy of state attempts to regulate the behaviour of the pregnant woman in the interest of the fetus. The prosecutions of feckless mothers who endanger their unborn child, or the taking into account of behaviour during pregnancy in order to assess suitability for parenthood, provide an interesting footnote to the great theme of the major shift in family law towards child protection. The issues, though, are of considerable jurisprudential note, and entail exactly the same juggling of interests which is encountered in all the other areas where medical advance, individual interest, and changing notions of family relationship come into creative and emotionally-charged conflict.

Note

1. [1985] 3 All ER 402 (HL).

1. Is anything left of parental rights?
Alexander McCall Smith

A persistent theme running through contemporary medico-legal discussion is that the concept of autonomy is all important. In this respect, medico-legal debate follows much other contemporary philosophical discussion, in which theories of morality have increasingly tended to be dominated by notions of autonomy.[1] Autonomy is all, and its denial, as one philosopher has suggested, amounts to a turning out of the lights.[2]

Illustrations of the role played by autonomy in medico-legal discussion come readily to hand. The most prominent, and indeed the most controversial of these, is the abortion debate. Those who argue for the ready availability of abortion on the basis of maternal choice frequently base their argument on what is, in their view, an unassailable proposition – the right of a woman to do with her body what she pleases. This argument is often dogmatically presented: in its most simplistic forms, little or no attention is paid to competing rights, nor to the issue of responsibility for others based on prior actings. Nor is the issue of personhood, potential or otherwise, of the fetus always adequately addressed. The argument may, of course, become more subtle, and some other derivative right may be promoted. Judith Jervis Thomson's classic defence of abortion is an example of this.[3] In her view, the pregnant woman has the right to act as a bad Samaritan to the fetus she is bearing. This right is not easily refuted, but it clearly depends on the acceptance of a right to express oneself in an uncharitable fashion, a right which is an unusual, but quite acceptable, aspect of autonomy.

Another area where the autonomy argument plays an important part is the debate on surrogacy. The decision to use reproductive capacity is taken by some to be a matter solely for the individual whose capacity is in question. Thus it becomes none of mine, or anybody else's business if a person chooses to carry a baby on behalf of another. It may be that surrogacy can be equiparated with prostitution (a strained analogy), but even if that is the case, then the defender of surrogacy may well be prepared (for consistency's sake) to be a defender of the right to engage in prostitution.

More significant, perhaps, is the role which autonomy has come to play in relation to life and death decisions affecting newborn infants. Here what we have seen is the extension of autonomy to cover not only those decisions which we make in relation to our own selves, but also to our newborn children. This is implicit in Michael Tooley's highly controversial analysis of infanticide, in which the non-existence of personhood in the new-born infant plunges the child into a position of vulnerability in relation to the fully autonomous parent.[4] In such circumstances, the power of the parent to determine whether or not the child lives is surely an inevitable concomitant of the recognition of parental autonomy. As Kuhse and Singer stress in their study of neonaticide, the persons whose lives are most directly affected by the birth of a handicapped child are the parents and it is therefore with them that the principal decision-making power should lie.[5] It is interesting to note the emphasis here. It is the effect of the child on the parents' lives which assumes considerable importance, and the impact of the infant on their ability to exercise their powers of autonomy therefore becomes a powerful factor in assessing its fate.

In all of these instances there is a tendency for the espousal of autonomy-based arguments to lead to a highly individualistic morality, in which the pursuit of self-interest outweighs other considerations. This flows from an important feature of autonomy as it is currently understood: being autonomous involves the right to act for oneself – to make one's own decisions. Yet most forms of action have an impact on others and in so far as autonomy allows freedom to act, it must be subject to the limitations imposed by the freedom of others to act, a freedom which flows from the recognition of their autonomy. Within the family, these limitations may be troublesome. If the autonomy of a child is recognized, then this recognition entails certain checks on the power of the parent to prevent the child from doing at least some of the things which an autonomous agent may wish to do. Conversely, the child's freedom of action may be restricted by parental interests which flow from the parents' own autonomy. The identifying of these various limitations may involve a delicate balancing of rights and interests, and this balance, as in the abortion argument, may often be elusive.

The ready invocation of the principle of autonomy entails other difficulties. Who enjoys, or should enjoy, autonomy? There may be no doubt over the autonomy of the adult possessed of his or her faculties: autonomy in such cases goes with personhood. But what about the special cases – the mentally handicapped person or the child? One approach to these cases is to say that autonomy is a quality which exists in all persons in the same measure, although the capacity to exercise it may be restricted. In the case of the child, then, autonomy is a quality which increases as the child matures and develops the capacity to act autonomously. Respect for the child's autonomy therefore requires that we should do nothing to hinder the development of the child as a fully autonomous person, capable of leading an autonomous life. This view of the autonomy of children places very specific responsibilities on the parent. It means that a child is not to be treated by the parent as a mere means: the child is an end in himself or herself. Everything that a parent does in respect of a child must then be for the benefit of that child, in the sense of enhancing the possibility of growth to full autonomy. This also means that as autonomy develops in the child, the child must be allowed to make decisions of his or her own, according to what he or she wants in life.

Where does this leave the parent – in practical terms? Is the parent merely a neutral 'guardian' of the child, whose sole function is to 'fill in' the undeveloped powers of autonomy of the child? If this is the case, then the parent's role is limited to that of a surrogate decision-maker, who decides on behalf of the child according to what that child might be expected to want were he or she in a position to make a decision. This is the opposite of authoritarian parenting and it could constitute an almost complete evisceration of the concept of parental rights. In what follows, I look at the whole question of the balance of child and parental rights in the medico-legal context and ask the question: 'What role, if any, do parents have in deciding on the medical treatment of their children?' The answer may strike some parents as surprising.

What rights should parents have?

Parenthood, as any parent will admit, is a drain financially, emotionally and physically. This is not to deny that there are compensations, which most parents would readily assert outweigh the burdens, and, of course, it hardly needs to be said that on socio-biological grounds parenthood is an overwhelmingly positive phenomenon. Yet for most people the decision to reproduce is not a deeply-reasoned one. The urge to have children is instinctive, and this is often enough in itself to set the process going. The feeling of being bereft which is frequently reported by those suffering from infertility is powerful enough evidence of the reality and strength of the urge to have children. So, although people may make a conscious decision to have children (expressed, with elegant irony in Paul Ramsey's phrase, 'Shall we reproduce?') the act of becoming a parent is not one which is the same as, say, a decision to become a member of a political party. It is a decision which usually entails responsibilities of a different sort from those which flow from many other decisions which we might make in our lives. In many respects, then, parenthood is a form of *status responsibility*, a form of responsibility in which moral obligations flow from the mere *being* of something. This type of responsibility differs in many important ways from responsibility based on the prior free exercise of choice.

A number of basic duties flow from the status of being a parent. The principal of these is the duty of protection, a duty which is based on the vulnerability of the child.[6] Other duties emerge as the child grows up, including a duty to educate and to provide the child with such opportunities for self-enhancement which are reasonably available to the parent. All of these duties, including the basic duty to protect, could be subsumed under the aegis of an overriding duty *to care and provide for the child*, and this duty in turn could be attributed, if one wants to couch it in terms of autonomy, to the duty to respect the child's growing autonomy.

It is important to note that these basic parental duties are, in the typical western jurisdiction at least, non-negotiable. It is not open for a parent to say: I accept that I must feed my child, but I don't accept that I have any duty to educate him or her. The response to that would be to say that a failure to educate is a gross dereliction of parental duty, at least in our society, where education is considered a right exigible both against parents and the community. The way in which we define parental duties is therefore fashioned in large measure by goals which are held desirable by society at large. Unlike moral obligations imposed on the basis of individual actings, where the conduct and motives of the individual may determine the nature and extent of the obligation, status responsibilities of this sort are of a very general nature and inevitably lend themselves to broad expression. It is rarely possible to opt out of a status obligation principally because of the social purpose which a status obligation is designed to serve.

The fact that parenthood is a matter of status has a profound influence on the way in which we have to consider parental rights. The Hohfeldian analysis of rights, which sets out to relate rights to duties, holds in essence that for every duty there exists a correlative right. Thus if I have a duty not to harm you in some way, then you have a corresponding right not to be harmed. For our present purposes, if emphasis is to be placed on parental duties, then equal attention must be placed on parental rights. But it does not really work that way in every case, particularly in the case of status obligations. A duty may give rise to a right, but this right may not always involve some benefit to the person on whom the duty rests: it may be no more than a right against the world not to be prevented from carrying out the duty. Status obligations may impose more duties than they do rights. A parent may have a duty to protect his or her child, but may have no right to expect reciprocal protection from the child at some later point. Some legal traditions impose upon children a duty to aliment their indigent parents when they are in a position to do so, but this is by no means accepted in every legal system. The child, of course, has an absolute right to expect aliment until such time as it is capable of supporting itself. It would seem, then, that what is absent from certain status obligations is an element of *reciprocity*. There is no theoretical reason, then, why parental rights should have to correspond in form to the duties which parents are obliged to accept.

Should a parent then have any rights at all? This question is not as absurd as it might sound. If one examines the history of the concept of parental rights as it has been interpreted both in English and in Scots law this century, a clear picture emerges of the gradual erosion of the whole notion that parents have any meaningful rights over their children.[7] The extreme, *patria potestas*-type notion of the nineteenth century, in which the autocratic father exercised extensive powers of direction over the lives of his children (and, to an extent, over the life of his wife) appeared increasingly anachronistic in the twentieth century. The concept of parental rights came to be not totally disapproved of, but nevertheless was subjected to increasing limitations, the effect of which was to enhance the area of autonomy of the child. This process has not necessarily been the product of a hostile view of parental rights in general, but has resulted more from the growing attraction for the courts of the idea that what counts more than anything else is the best interests of the child. In the landmark decision in *Gillick v. West Norfolk and Wisbech Area Health Authority*,[8] however, the House of Lords confronted the issue head on and the majority of judges further endorsed the waning of parental rights in the face of contemporary views of the competence of minors to make decisions relating to their personal lives.

The diminution of parental rights has not gone unopposed and

Is anything left of parental rights?

there has been, in fact, a strong reaction against what has been seen as a weakening of family integrity. The work of Goldstein, Freud and Solnit[9] was particularly influential in this movement, arguing in favour of family autonomy and privacy in the face of state interventionism. In spite of these arguments, and in spite of the political support they attracted, the courts (at least in Britain) seem to have remained firmly wedded to the principle that what matters most is the welfare or the best interests of the child. So strong has the best interests principle become that the question needs to be addressed as to whether there is anything left of parental rights — perhaps a category of *parent-centred* parental rights which has survived the growing legal and philosophical acceptance of the autonomy of children. If this category exists, does it or should it include any rights over the medical welfare of the child?

The category of parent-centred rights

The task of singling out special areas which could be seen as parent-centred rights is not simple. The cause of this difficulty is the problems which will be encountered if one tries to distinguish the various components of a parent's overall parenting right over that child. The overarching right is undoubtedly that of custody, and from this flows a great variety of derivative rights (the right to control the child's associations with others, the right to choose education, the right to dictate various matters from diet to religion). Some of these are clearly 'child-centred parental rights', that is, rights to be exercised for the benefit of the child; others are parent-centred. A child-centred parental right finds its justification in the furtherance of the child's best interests, or the child's welfare. The parental right to dictate the hours during which a child may be out of the house, for example, is a child-centred right, being intended to protect the child from harm. By contrast, the right to insist on the form of a child's religious upbringing, or the right to choose (within limits set by the state) the way in which the child is educated are both examples of parent-centred rights. What these last two examples have in common is that they touch upon the parental response to the basic moral issue of *what sort of child they wish to raise*.

The main significance of a right being categorized as parent-centred would appear to be that the parent has a wide range of discretion to pursue goals which society as a whole might find undesirable, but which it will tolerate. The purpose of such rights is therefore parent-directed; part of their reason for existence is the fact that they reflect something to which the parent is entitled by virtue of being a parent. The right to the society of the child is a parental right, and it is appropriately considered as a parent-centred right, and yet it has nothing to do with any consideration of the welfare of the child. This right is accorded to thoroughly disagreeable (though not violent) parents in exactly the same way as it is accorded to those who are more congenial company from the child's point of view.

One way then of distinguishing between parent-centred rights and others is to identify who is the beneficiary of the right. We might take the parental right to a child's society as an example: it is true that a child benefits from the society of its parents, but that fact surely is grounds for asserting the *child*'s right to parental society, which is another right altogether. In the case of a parental right to a child's society, any infringement of the right deprives the parent of a benefit. Similarly, with the right to instil religious values in a child, the infringement of such a right involves distress to the parent, not necessarily to the child. This view far from reflects current orthodoxy, in that many commentators on parental rights argue that the whole and exclusive point of parental rights is to serve the interest of the children. This appears not to be true in relation to these rights, in which self-serving parental wishes are taken into account.

Two factors which weaken any parental rights are (i) a threat to the welfare of the child, and (ii) the growth of the child's right to autonomy. The pursuit by a parent of an educational theory which imposed intolerable physical stress on the child would justify social intervention in exactly the same way as would the conduct of an ill-tempered and violent parent. The second factor has the effect of diminishing the strength of a right over time. The development within a child of moral judgement and the ability to make an independent assessment of moral problems affects the right of a parent to dictate moral education. Equally, growth to social independence may be said to weaken the parental right to the child's society. These rights are therefore not totally unassailable; they weaken with time and they may be taken from parents in certain circumstances.

The classification of medical rights

If it is accepted that some rights allow parents a wide area of discretion and have, as their rationale, the interest of the parent rather than of the child, then the question arises as to which rights (other than those mentioned above) might be placed in this category. In particular, the question should be addressed as to whether there is any justification for so classifying parental rights to determine the medical treatment of children.

Parents may be called upon to make decisions in relation to the medical treatment of their children in widely varying circumstances. This process might now begin even at the pre-natal stage, where decisions may have to be made about the termination of a pregnancy where there is evidence of handicap of some sort. Here the distinction between the child- and parent-centred right approach is starkly evident. If one takes the view that the right here is parent-centred, then greater rather than lesser freedom should be accorded to parents in this situation. The parent-centred element in such a right suggests that it is proper for the parents to consider here their own interests, and that if the birth of a child suffering from a particular form of handicap would have an unacceptable effect on their own lives, then they are entitled to exercise their discretion in favour of preventing the birth of that child. This position, in effect, is one which the majority of those who accept abortion would probably endorse.

The same exercise of parental discretion may, of course, be described in a different, less parent-centred way. The decision to terminate a pregnancy in such a case might be viewed as the exercise of a child-centred right; the principal consideration being the unacceptable quality of life which the child would be obliged to endure if the parental right to choose abortion were not to be exercised. Where the focus lies may thus vary, depending on what parental motives are.

The rights of fetuses are, however, a difficult, and perhaps distracting case. If we turn to the newborn, parents may again be asked to decide difficult issues of treatment alternatives. There are some who see parental decisions as to the treatment or non-treatment of handicapped children here as being a matter exclusively for the parents. This appears to have been the case in the circumstances leading up to the prosecution in the case of *R. v. Arthur*,[10] where parental wishes were stated by the paediatrician to be the grounds for the provision of nursing care only. Yet in the case of *Re B*,[11] which involved a parental decision not to pursue treatment in a case of a Down's syndrome infant suffering from a surgically correctable condition, any parental right to make such a choice in such a case was firmly denied. This judgement unambiguously emphasized the best interest of the child in the face of a life-threatening parental decision.

In some United States cases, however, the parental autonomy argument has had different results, most notoriously in the widely-criticized case of *Re Phillip B.*,[12] where parents vetoed surgery on a mentally handicapped boy who could have enjoyed many years of life before dying of heart disease.

It is no surprise then to see the courts in cases such as *Re B* setting firm limits to any parental right over the life and death of a child. It is significant, though, that these limitations have had to be set in the context of infants, undoubtedly the most vulnerable group among children. In spite of such arguments advanced for a parental right of life or death the attitude of the criminal law has remained consistent in its refusal to countenance life-threatening child neglect, and here at least can be identified a clear limit to any parental right to reject treatment. Nor will doctors wishing to treat a child find themselves without support from the state: a parent who, for example, declines to authorize a blood transfusion for a child facing death without such treatment will find that the state is ready to intervene by an assumption of parental rights. The justification for intervention in the face of parental opposition is said to be the primacy of the child's welfare over any parental right to veto treatment.

This is, of course, an extreme case; the child's right to life is an extremely 'strong right', taken very seriously by the law. In many other circumstances there may be no threat to the child's life, and the motivation for treatment is a lesser, though still important, interest; namely, that of good health. The question that needs to be addressed here is the extent to which the welfare principle is capable of overruling parental rights, even where parental conduct poses no threat to the life of the child. A parent might, for example, pursue a dietary enthusiasm which will deny the child a balanced diet. This may have no effect on the child's survival, but may nonetheless have some impact on, say, growth rate. Is what the parent is doing in such a case within the range of acceptable parental discretion, or is it a course of action in which intervention is appropriate? An initial, practical observation has to be made here. Other than in the case of the child too young to protest an opinion, or in the case of the mentally handicapped child, this issue is likely to arise only where the relationship between the child has broken down so completely that the child has sought external help, or where the child has involved, through medical consultation, some third party, possibly a doctor or nurse. The issue of intervention can therefore arise both where there is a child who is fundamentally in conflict with parents and therefore possibly of an age where parental rights are already diminished, and also in cases where the child is caught in between parents and outsiders. In the latter case, the rights and wrongs of intervention must be seen in the context of a child/parent relationship that is still a viable proposition. Different considerations may apply in each of these cases.

The area in which this issue has been mostly hotly contested is undoubtedly that of contraception. The *Gillick* decision[13] answers the question of whether a minor can be given contraception without parental consent, but how far can the decision in this case be generalized to provide guidance on the general issue of the competence of the parent to veto other forms of medical intervention? On a restrictive view of *Gillick* all that the decision actually says is that a minor who is sufficiently mature to understand contraceptive treatment may agree to the provision of such treatment provided that the doctor agrees to provide it on this basis. No *right* to such treatment is proposed, nor does the decision state that minors have a general right to make all medical decisions relating to themselves. This prompts the question: is there anything in the nature of contraception itself which legitimizes its administration without parental consent?

The obvious and immediate purpose of contraception may be to prevent pregnancy, but behind this there may lie the objectives of (i) protection of the health of a person for whom child-bearing would be dangerous; (ii) the prevention of the birth of a child who could not be looked after by the mother, or who is not wanted for whatever reason; or (iii) the facilitation of sexual self-fulfilment. These considerations are frequently bound up with one another, and, in the case of the unmarried young girl, the main consideration is probably going to be the avoidance of a pregnancy which would be highly disruptive socially and emotionally. Contraception is not provided in such a case as a protection against a life-threatning condition, it is simply a means of protecting against an event which would take a considerable psychological and practical toll.

It is possible to take this view of it no matter what is thought about the fact of sexual activity at this stage of life. A person who disapproves of fourteen- or fifteen-year-old girls engaging in sexual intercourse may do so from a variety of standpoints, but this disapproval need not, as in the case of Mrs Gillick, and in the case of at least a proportion of the judges who decided the matter in the various stages of its passage through the courts, entail a refusal to endorse the ready availability of something which will act as a prophylactic against making matters worse. The provision of contraception can be quite easily seen then as a form of damage limitation exercise.

If this view is taken, then contraception may be viewed either as a form of preventative treatment (of much the same nature as an inoculation), or it may even be considered to be a form of treatment which is designed to limit the extent of damage which has already been caused (the onset of the sexual relationship). If it is seen as either of these, then it should surely be capable of being subsumed within the category of treatments to which Lord Fraser in his judgement thought it would be absurd for a child not to be able to give consent (the setting of a broken arm or the treating of a minor injury). Of course, if contraception is seen as a 'life-style question', in which moral considerations play a powerful role, then parental rights to be involved in the treatment decision could be very much greater. For some of the judges in the House of Lords stage of *Gillick*, this is precisely what contraception was, but the opposite view has ultimately prevailed, at least for English law.

An interesting comparison may be made with the much more extensive judicial consideration which this matter has received in the United States. In a number of cases, the courts have considered both at State and Supreme Court level the constitutional acceptability of legislation seeking to restrict the access that young people have to contraception. The issue has been framed in fundamentally different terms in the United States, with the emphasis being on the rights of the child to privacy in respect of reproductive decisions. The matter has therefore not been one of ability to consent to medical decisions, but has turned upon the protection of the minor's right to make certain choices. This was the approach adopted, for example, in the important case of *Carey v. Population Services International*,[14] in which the Supreme Court struck down New York legislation penalizing the provision of contraception to minors. Not all American decisions go this far in recognizing the rights of the minor to self determination, but there is nonetheless a clear line of decisions endorsing this approach. *Planned Parenthood of Missouri v. Danforth*[15] and similar decisions provide examples, then, of how even if one views a treatment decision as being a lifestyle matter, it is still possible to regard it as being a matter for the minor alone.

Abortion is another area where the question of parental rights has been an issue. The matter came before the courts in the United

Kingdom in *Re P (a Minor)*[16] in 1982, a case in which a fifteen-year-old girl wished to proceed with an abortion in the face of parental wishes to the contrary. The decision went in the girl's favour, essentially on the grounds that she understood the procedure and wanted it. This case, although the only one of its type, is in harmony with other cases in which men have attempted to prevent the abortion of a fetus which they fathered (*Paton v. British Pregnancy Advisory Services*;[17] *C. v. S.*[18]).In neither of the latter two cases was minority an issue, but the principle of the maternal focus of the abortion decision was strongly endorsed.

How is the decision to undergo an abortion to be categorized? Are we to consider it in the same light as the treatment of a physical injury (Lord Fraser's 'broken arm category'[19]),or is it something more? In favour of the treatment approach is the fact that legal abortion under the terms of the Abortion Act 1967 is likely to be a therapeutic matter, intended to protect the minor from serious harm to physical or psychological health. As such, it can be argued that it is properly classed with decisions relating to the treatment of injury or the like. Many would contest this hotly. It could be argued that submission to abortion is a matter of profound moral significance. If parents cannot advise on such a momentous step, the consequences of which may be long-lasting, then is there any moral issue left on which they may have the right to advise? We might consider it from the point of view of a parent who is a member of the Roman Catholic Church. Such a person may consider abortion to be nothing short of murder, and the right to prevent a child from taking that step should be considered a fundamental parental right. It would require a high degree of insensitivity to deny the genuine moral concern in such a case, but it would seem that parental rights now do in fact stop short of allowing the parent to act in such a case.

With both examples discussed so far – contraception and abortion – it would seem that parental rights to intervene are severely restricted. Both of these instances are examples of treatment which can be viewed as procedures which either seek to prevent a risk to health or seek to prevent its deterioration. Here, at least, the minor's wishes prevail, and the doctor can pursue goals which are at odds with parental wishes. Neither of them necessarily falls into the category of treatment required to prevent the occurrence of a life-threatening event, but they both involve potentially serious consequences. Does this mean that parental rights are, somewhat surprisingly, excluded in those cases where weighty medical decisions are to be made and recognized only where the exercise of parental discretion would have little impact one way or the other? The thrust of recent court decisions on the treatment of minors suggests that this is undoubtedly the current view.

It would seem that the rise of the welfare principle has resulted in the development of a concept of child health which is objectively determined, according to medical and social orthodoxy, and that this is the standard against which parental attitudes are to be measured. This principle of child welfare admits of the medical self-determination of the child as long as the child's decisions are not at variance with what the welfare principle deems to be desirable; where there is a serious conflict between what the minor wants to do and what the welfare principle would suggest is the best course of action, then the latter will probably be of greater weight.

Parental rights to determine treatment of the minor are not necessarily excluded by the welfare principle, but it is clear that such rights are now subservient and potentially relegated to a very small area of operation once one has effectively excluded them from the area of reproductive decisions and life-threatening conditions. What role, then, does the parent still have in determining the medical welfare of the child? Obviously day-to-day parental discretion continues to be exercised. The parent will decide when the child is to be taken to the doctor or the dentist, and, once there, is obviously involved in treatment decisions. There is still a prima facie right to veto treatment, even if a life-threatening condition is diagnosed, but this right is subject to being overruled. In the case already mentioned, where a parent refuses a blood transfusion for an injured child for whose survival this transfusion is essential, the parent's attempt to exercise a right of veto may be frustrated either through the non-consensual administration of the treatment (on the principle of necessity[20]) or through the taking of legal steps by social welfare authorities to give them power to authorize treatment (for example, in Scotland, through the assumption of parental rights under the Social Work (Scotland) Act 1968). Where the condition is not life-threatening, the position is somewhat more ambiguous. A child who suffers from a deformity (for example, a cleft palate) may benefit from corrective surgery; but what is the position if a parent elects to veto surgery for whatever reason, possibly religious?[21] Or what is the position if a parent should decline to allow treatment for a psychiatric condition from which the child suffers? The welfare principle provides strong grounds here for intervention, but whether such intervention would be allowed by the courts is not clear. In most cases, the medical personnel involved would want so settle the issue through persuasion; but in the rare stubborn case this might fail and professional views may remain at odds with parental views as to what is best for the child.

In principle, it is difficult to see how parental rights to refuse treatment could be supported in such cases. Once there is an acceptance of the welfare concept, then the fact that treatment is in the child's best interests according to that concept should be the sole determination of the matter unless, and this is a very significant exception, it is accepted that a parent-centred right should be recognized here. Parent-centred rights in the area of medical treatment, however, have been rejected in the area of reproduction and life-or-death treatment, so why should they be recognized in this context? One answer is to say that the parent-centred aspect of the right can be acknowledged because the harm caused to the child is less significant than the harm caused to the parent by the denial of his or her right to determine the treatment of the child. An objection to this argument is that there will be very few cases in which this balancing of harms will result in a decision in favour of the parent, given current attitudes towards parenting in western societies. There may have been a time when it was regarded as reasonable that parents should wish to bring up children reflecting their values and behaving as they, the parents, would wish to see them behave. Today, though, the emphasis on personal autonomy is applied to the very youngest, and the role of the parent is widely seen as being that of serving the growth of this autonomy. The child's interest, therefore, is likely to 'trump' the parental interest in almost every case, at least in the area of medical treatment if not in every other context.

In giving this degree of recognition to the child's interest, the law automatically increases the possibility of intervention in parent/child matters and vastly extends its protective role in relation to children. This process has happened in many countries in a gradual way and has sometimes led to results which have caused public concern. It may be that the legal erosion of parental rights is not a development which society as a whole is ready to accept without certain misgivings, and that there remain areas of parent/child relations where the widely accepted child-autonomy view of parenting referred to above encounters resistance. A good example of this is provided by the example of child sexual abuse, a major problem of which the public has only comparatively recently become aware. Here parental rights have been vigorously asserted in the face of well-meant intervention by doctors and social workers. The child welfare principle is uncontested: society has a right to protect all children against sexual abuse. Yet attempts to ensure that abuse is prevented or that the effects of past abuse be treated, have raised issues of parental rights. Where sexual abuse is suspected, clinical examination may be the only way of determining whether this has occurred, and yet such examination involves issues of parental rights. In the Cleveland case, in which many children were subjected to clinical examination without parental consent, the rights of parents to be consulted were later stressed, and this led in due course to the making of legislative provision for sanctioning by the courts of such examinations. Such legislation at least puts the matter beyond legal doubt: parental views, though to be taken into account, are still subject to the state's interest in determining whether a child has been abused. Ultimately, in this context then, parental rights yield to the interests of the child in not being subjected to psychologically and physically damaging conduct at the hands of others.

The developments outlined above seem to suggest that parental rights in relation to medical treatment might now be re-defined as being 'consultative rights'. A parent has a right to be informed of treatment which is proposed for his or her child, but ultimately the question of what treatment is given will be determined on the basis of what medical opinion, as endorsed by the courts, considers best for that child. Although the state may be slow to invoke powers to authorize treatment in the face of parental objection, those powers are all in place, whether in the form of legislation allowing the assumption of parental powers or in the shape of common law recognition of the minor's own right to consent to treatment, the court's right to authorize treatment, or the doctor's right to proceed on the grounds of necessity. The gradual demotion of parental rights in this area may be viewed as another example of the gradually encroaching power of the interventionist state in the area of the bringing up of children. Viewed from another angle it is a liberation from the outmoded autocracy of powerful adults over vulnerable children. This latter view is the more sympathetic, kinder view, and its legal endorsement is, on balance, welcome.

Notes

1. For an analysis of the broad role played by the concept of autonomy in contemporary moral philosophy, see Dworkin, *The Theory and Practice of Autonomy*, Cambridge: Cambridge University Press, 1988, chapter 1.
2. Haworth, *Autonomy: an essay in philosophical psychology and ethics*, New Haven: Yale University Press, 1986.
3. Thomson, *Rights, Restitution and Risk*, Cambridge, Mass: Harvard University Press, 1986, p. 1.
4. Tooley, *Abortion and infanticide*, Oxford, Clarendon Press, 1983.
5. Kuhse and Singer, *Should the baby live?* Oxford: Oxford University Press, 1985.
6. The role of vulnerability as a source of moral obligations to others has been explored and developed by Robert Goodin in his *Protecting the vulnerable*, Chicago: University of Chicago Press, 1985.
7. There is a wealth of literature on the subject. For a good survey, which concentrates on the implications of the *Gillick* case (n.8, *infra*), see Bainham, 'The balance of power in family decisions' 45 *Cambridge Law Journal* (1986), 262.
8. [1985] 3 All ER 402, HL.
9. Goldstein, Freud and Solnit, *Beyond the best interests of the child*, London, Burnett Books, 1979. For a useful survey of the judicial and political response to these arguments, see Dickens, 'The modern function and limits of parental rights' 97 *Law Quarterly Review* (1981), 462.
10. [1981] 1 WLR 1421.
11. (1981) *The Times*, 6 Nov., 1. This case has been widely discussed. See, for example, Brahams, 'Putting *Arthur*'s case in perspective' [1986] Crim LR 387. The primacy of the best interests of the child, together with the competence of medical staff to determine what such interests are (at least in the case of a terminally ill child) are similarly endorsed in *Re C (a minor)* [1989] 2 All ER 782.
12. 156 Cal. Rept. 48 (1979); cert. den. 100 S.Ct. 1597 (1980).
13. Note 8, *supra*.
14. 431 US 678 (1977).
15. 428 US 52 (1976).
16. (1982) LGR 301. See Mason, *Medico-legal aspects of reproduction and parenthood*, Aldershot: Dartmouth, 1990, p. 49.
17. [1979] QB 276.
18. [1988] QB 135.
19. Discussed by Cusine, at p. 85, *infra*.

20. The application of the necessity principle has been much strengthened by the broad view taken of it by the House of Lords in F. v. *West Berkshire Health Authority* [1989] 2 WLR 1025. The position in Scotland over the application of the necessity principle in the civil context remains, however, curiously opaque. A search for judicial authority on necessity as a defence to a civil claim reveals nothing of substance although, on principle, necessity, constituting a justification, would exclude *culpa*.
21. American cases touching upon this issue are discussed by Meyers, p. 74, *infra*.

2. Reproductive technology and the 'new' family
Bernard M. Dickens

Addressing the social phenomenon of the 'new' family requires at least summary consideration of families in classical understanding. As conventionally perceived, families were associations of persons related genetically or by marriage and identified by their interaction and affinity and usually their names. The family history or tree was a genetic and marital line traceable back through earlier generations, which in western cultures and cultures of many other regions bore the name of the male line. That is, male-centred surnames such as 'Johnson', 'Peterson', 'McDonald' and 'O'Sullivan' have no female equivalent surnames, and are comparable to aristocratic names of feudal origin traceable to tenure of landed estates, shown in members of the peerage such as Lords being 'of' somewhere. A man, as opposed to a woman, was identified with his family location, to which he brought his wife from her father's home.

Families were linked not just by genetics and affinity, however, but also by lawful succession. History as taught in lower school years is a succession of the lives of kings and related nobility, from which illegitimate or bastard offspring are excluded or hinted at darkly. The history of the commoner was not recorded because, possessing nothing but perhaps a personal name to pass on, the common person had no need to document a line of legal succession. Marriages of commoners did not have to be marked by rituals of church and state, because they were of only local relevance. A common marriage was often marked, particularly in pre-literate societies, by an occasion of eating and drinking alcohol, more noteworthy in populations accustomed to plain foods hard earned from the land, hunting or trapping, rendering a feast a locally memorable event that established who was sexually tied to whom and unavailable to others.

In law, the children of such unions were 'illegitimate' or bastards, a word that today remains a degrading epithet. The description of an 'illegitimate child' is fading in sensitive discussion, but for long it had stigmatized the offspring of an illicit union in ways that far exceeded forfeiture of inheritance from, and through, a father and often through a mother. The expression 'child' in law was often limited to mean a legitimate child.[1] The idea of an illegitimate child, meaning one who, by law, should not be a child, makes little sense. Such children were the children of illegitimate parents, meaning people who, by law, should not have shared the child's parentage, because, for instance, they were legally unmarried or married to others. Describing the child by reference to the marital status of the parents further disadvantaged the victim, even when the parents lived in a cohesive, mutually faithful but unmarried union. Such 'Common Law' unions had an ambivalent status in imperial times when, in the cultures of colonized lands, they were often in full conformity with the prevailing customary law. They frequently had a social legitimacy too, throughout the empire, although according to the values not of the lawyer but of the sociologist or anthropologist.

The history of common folk is largely unrecorded. The family histories that we can trace through public and other legal records, including church records,[2] are histories of succession to male-owned land, titles and other possessions through genetically coherent lines. A classical family was an association of related people among whom property was legally transferred, through marriage, reproduction of children and death, predominantly through a male line of succession.

Against this setting, the modern or 'new' family may appear quite different. The underlying concept of 'property' itself is different, the new property consisting in professional qualifications and similar credentials and experience through which a livelihood can be earned, credit ratings, mortgaged land and other real estate held in condominium, co-operative and other contractual agreements. Children's succession to such property is guaranteed as much by legislation, including landlord and tenant Acts, as by exercise of private power.[3] Similarly, now that, related to raised standards of public and private health care, divorce has replaced early death as the event that ends marriage, and remarriage is more common, genetic coherence in families is more difficult to perceive and trace. Families may be composed of husband and wife, her children, his children and their children. Further, the single-parent family, usually but not invariably based on a woman, is an established fact.[4] A high percentage of children will spend part of their infancy, childhood and adolescence, if not its entire duration, in single-parent families.[5]

The reproductive technologies fit into this setting, but did not create it and should not be over-emphasized as the socially destabilizing force that achieved the transition from the order and genetic coherence of the conventionally perceived family to the 'new' family founded on the unstable features of transitory human associations, unclear or anonymous genetic links, intangible property concepts, and the vanishing significance of male succession. The new reproductive technologies are opposed, however, by at least two diametrically opposed forces. One is that of traditional religion, which has sanctified the conventionally composed family as 'the Basic Unit of Society' and regards the random mixing of gametes (sperm and ova) implicated in several techniques used to overcome infertility as deliberately destructive of society and of family sentiments. This view implies that what parents most love in their children are their own genes and prospects of genetic immortality, and that what inspires children's affection and defines their identity is their genetic origin. Another force is that of radical feminism, which sees modern reproductive technology as a male conspiracy to displace and devalue the social, domestic and economic status of women by using them as depersonalized, interchangeable walking incubators, and eventually to build artificial wombs through which men can gestate their sons without having to know women in either biblical or social senses.[6]

Infertility

The reproductive technologies are heavily goal-oriented, being directed to the achievement of children and increasingly measuring their success in terms not simply of pregnancies initiated[7] but of 'take home babies'. Although their development has been a response to infertility, feminist critics have claimed that the stigmatization of infertility is itself a contrivance or psychological construct of peddlers of prospective technological 'fixes'.[8] Anthropological and other observers of societies may find the distress of infertility more historic, spontaneous and authentic, but traditional societies have associated infertility with the failure of women, and rendered it a ground of divorce. Reproductive technologies approach individuals at a basic level of their capacity to produce gametes capable of creating healthy babies, and women as capable of gestating and delivering them safely.

Although capacity to conceive and bear children was the precondition of classical or conventional family-building, the infertile are not necessarily childless. Primary or permanent infertility is distinguishable from secondary infertility.[9] The latter affects those whose earlier fertility may have been indicated in the birth or conception of children but who are unable at some stage in their lives to conceive the children they want and see them come to full gestation and birth. The full extent of infertility is not known because many infertile people do not seek to conceive children, especially those affected by secondary infertility who may have completed building families to their satisfaction. Some, indeed, unaware of the onset of infertility, conscientiously practice contraception and have had sterilization or vasectomy procedures in order to terminate a supposed reproductive capacity that others struggle to achieve, and that those undergoing these procedures may subsequently struggle to regain.

Causes of infertility are various, and not necessarily pathological.[10] Clearly, disease-derived infertility and that occasioned by surgery or prescribed medical treatment is associated with adverse health, and that caused by a toxic or otherwise harmful work or residential environment is artificially induced, but much results from lifestyle. Fertility decreases naturally with age, and the later in life reproduction is sought, the more difficult it will be to achieve. With postponed marriage, due perhaps to the pursuit of advanced education or of career goals, and with the advent of a second or later marriage in which children are wanted, the hope to have children may arise, or return, later in life than was once usual.

The extent of infertility in a community is to some significant degree determined as a function of its definition. Medical, demographic and social definitions do not necessarily coincide, but a conventional test of infertility had until recently been failure to initiate and to retain a pregnancy during twenty-four months of regular sexual intercourse without contraceptive protection. A more recent test, however, is such failure during twelve months. The newer test may reflect the impatience of patients of relatively advanced reproductive age to receive treatment, particularly when it is paid for by a governmental or other third-party subscribed health insurance plan, or the willingness of health professionals to initiate treatment on reliable evidence, but not necessarily an overwhelmingly strong case, of infertility. Clearly, more will be infertile on a twelve than a twenty-four month test. The generally expressed estimate that one couple in six (some claim five) of reproductive age seeking to conceive is infertile must be interpreted against the background of applicable definitions and social conditions that determine the likelihood that occasions to test fertility will arise.

Within the functional category of the infertile may be included some who are fertile. 'Unexplained infertility' is an increasingly common diagnosis health professionals make when two apparently fertile people join in an infertile union; that is, two people who are apparently able to have children with other partners, and may already have done so, but not with each other due, for instance, to a woman's allergic reaction to her partner's sperm. Further, the category may include women able to conceive but not to retain pregnancy. Chronic spontaneous abortion is an indicator of infertility notwithstanding the woman's ovulation and normal conception, due for instance to uterine dysfunction causing premature expulsion of uterine contents. A sizeable component of the infertile is composed of those whose naturally conceived children would be at high risk to suffer severe genetic defects. Dysgenic risk is a conscientious cause of functional infertility that gamete donation may overcome, although alternatives exist. Couples whose children are at high risk to suffer, for instance, Tay Sachs disease, may initiate pregnancy naturally and rely on prenatal genetic diagnosis to assess fetal status. Female fetuses will either be unaffected or have the same carrier status as their mothers. Male fetuses will either be unaffected or affected and highly liable to die after two or so years of painful and distressed life. These latter pregnancies can be terminated under the laws of most countries.[11]

It is interesting to observe how unsympathetic traditional institutions are towards infertility. They may point to the contribution sexually transmitted diseases make to its volume, or the recklessness of people who had voluntary sterilizations or vasectomies in one relationship and want them reversed or overcome in later unions, with no acknowledgement of how changed circumstances can reflect the natural progression of life, including family life. Public health agencies such as governmental health departments frequently consider infertility treatment to be such a low priority that, while appropriately cautious of high-technology, high-cost procedures to accommodate relatively few applicants, they overlook how modest expenditures on educational and preventive programmes might reap a rich return in reproductive health maintenance and promotion. Similarly, while churches pay lip-service to the infertile through platitudes of concern, their adherence to conservative social values is frequently rationalized through biblical and similarly pious condemnations of the reproductive technologies. Accusing reproductive technologists of assuming a divine role in acting aggressively to achieve pregnancy, they assume a divine role in acting to prevent or inhibit it. Invoking the imperative to be fruitful and multiply to condemn contraception and sterilization, they fashion concepts of nature to condemn reproductive technologies that would promote the births of wanted children as being unnatural. The Roman Catholic church, led by elderly celibate men who have no experience of guiltless sex,[12] has been particularly assertive to condemn young couples whose hopes to have children depend on these techniques, and its Congregation for the Doctrine of the Faith has commanded that secular politicians be obedient to its clerical vision.[13] The violence that is done not just to compassion but to the profession of being a pro-family church is rationalized through conservative genetic tests of what constitutes a legitimate family.

The Reproductive Technologies

The technologies that are available to enhance fertility and to overcome infertility by permitting those who seek them to have children to which they or their partners have made a genetic contribution can be explained to laypeople, meaning those who are not obstetricians, gynaecologists, endocrinologists or reproductive biologists, at different degrees of sophistication or abstraction.[14] For present purposes, a simplistic, technically primitive outline is all that is needed in order to explore some of the implications of the technologies for the legal structure of 'new' families. The methods in issue can be generally separated into:

a) Gamete transfer for *in vivo* fertilization;
b) *In vitro* fertilization; and
c) Surrogate motherhood.

a) Gamete transfer for in vivo fertilization

Until recently, this procedure was generally known as Artificial Insemination by Donor (AID), but this name has now been superseded by Therapeutic Donor Insemination (TDI), for two reasons. The first is that the acronym AID is too close for comfort and clarity to AIDS, acquired immunodeficiency syndrome. The other, less compelling reason, is that 'insemination by donor' appears limited to donation of semen or sperm, whereas it is now possible for ova to be donated and fertilized by the partner of the recipient. The expression TDI may still suggest donation of semen or sperm rather than of ova, but the description emphasizes therapeutic donation and allows insemination to be through a recipient's partner or a third party donor. The technique permits conception by placing donated sperm in a woman's reproductive system, and also by so placing her partner's sperm when, for instance, he is impotent or a low sperm count requires that his sperm be accumulated or treated before insemination, the procedure sometimes being called Artificial Insemination by Husband (AIH). Alternatively, a donated ovum can be placed *in vivo* for natural insemination by a partner, or donated ova and sperm may be so placed for *in vivo* fertilization. This coincides with a process called Gamete Interfallopian Transfer (GIFT), which is a variant of *in vitro* fertilization.

b) In vitro fertilization (IVF)

This procedure arose to overcome obstacles to natural fertilization, such as when scarred or otherwise damaged and obstructed fallopian tubes, or missing tubes due, for instance, to congenital or surgical reasons, prevented sperm from travelling up the tubes to reach an ovum descending from an ovary. Where there was no natural bridge, IVF provided a type of helicopter service to permit transit of sperm to ova. The technique removed an ovum, or ova, and exposed it or them to the partner's sperm in a petrie dish, represented in the popular mind by a test tube. The world's first 'test-tube' baby, Louise Brown, born in July 1978 in England following pioneering work of the late Dr Patrick Steptoe and Dr Robert Edwards, was unremarkable, except for her *in vitro* conception, in being the genetic child of her social mother and father. Variants of IVF soon appeared, however, including employment of donated sperm, or ova, or both, and opening the way to implanting the *in vitro* fertilized pre-embryo into a woman who intended, on birth, to surrender the child to the custody of another, notably a gamete donor, in a surrogate motherhood arrangement. The variant of combining donated or 'own' gametes not in glass (*in vitro*) but in the natural *in vivo* setting produced GIFT, mentioned above. The reservations some feminist critics of IVF express are based on its physical and emotional effects on women and on its efficacy to date, rather than on its capacity to function to create families.

c) Surrogate motherhood (SM)

Perhaps the most apparently disruptive reproductive technology in terms of family functioning is SM, which may not be dependent on any technology at all. So-called 'partial' SM, in which a woman conceives and gestates her own genetic child, can be achieved by relatively unskilled use of a kitchen instrument such as a turkey-baster, perhaps but not necessarily at some slight risk to the woman, or by natural intercourse such as in condoned adultery.[15] 'Full' or 'total' SM arises when a woman receives a pre-embryo created from another woman's ovum, through IVF or *in vivo* fertilization and pre-embryo recovery by a process variously called lavage, flushing, washing or irrigation. Full SM is clearly dependent on medical techniques for creation or recovery of the pre-embryo and its insertion in the gestating mother. Early responses to SM were based on partial SM, before means of full SM were developed. In North America, the 1987 New Jersey *Baby* M case,[16] in which a gestating mother fought to retain if not custody of, then at least access to, her own genetic child born in a partial SM arrangement triggered twin responses. It publicized the pitfalls of SM by exposing the procedure working at its worst, and it added to the attractiveness of full SM, and in both cases showed the significance of screening potential gestating mothers. Full SM is not necessarily less controversial but, unlike partial SM, it results in a couple receiving a child that is the genetic child of both of them, in conformity with the most conservative model of family structure. The challenge to family values affects not the recipient couple, however, but the gestating mother. If she is unmarried, she completes pregnancy but has no child, as in stillbirth, if she is married her family experiences her pregnancy with only monetary payment or altruistic satisfaction as reward, and if she has children she may appear to them as a woman willing to give away her child. Above all, the practice seems to depend on the domestic dysfunction of facilitating a woman to have a child when she does not intend to rear it within her own family.

Family Issues in Gamete Transfer

Reproductive technologies are comparable to modern developments in social lifestyle that accommodate unmarried and serial married reproduction, in that they contribute to the creation of families in which children may be genetically unrelated to their social or psychological parents,[17] and in which children in the same households may not genetically have both or either such parents in common. Parenthood itself has become divisible into genealogical or genetic parenthood, gestational motherhood, and social or psychological parenthood, and different people may discharge the functions of such parenthood regarding the same child. To the historic functions of step-parenthood, adoptive parenthood and foster-parenthood the reproductive technologies have added a small number of pre-natal variants. In light of our recorded experience of the different post-natal domestic environments in which children may be reared, perhaps we should not over-react to the addition of variants to children's pre-natal origins. Speculative claims that children of the reproductive technologies may suffer from genealogical bewilderment and disorientation remain unproven.[18]

Legal problems have arisen from gamete donation, however, that have to be addressed. The selection of donors raises issues, for instance, not simply of the health professionals who make selections thereby influencing the future genetic composition of families and society in conscious or unconscious fulfillment of eugenic blueprints, but of the screening standards and criteria they apply. A legal duty of care is owed to recipients of donated gametes to ensure that the gametes have been selected and the donors tested according to prevailing standards of knowledge and competence, in order to ensure that recipients will not themselves contract disorders through acceptance of the gametes and that the children they thereby conceive will be at no more risk to suffer genetic handicaps than exists in natural reproduction. More problematic is the claim a child would have if a gamete donor was negligently selected or tested and contributed deleterious genes that result in the child's handicap.[19]

Classification of the child's claim in this circumstance poses legal problems. The claim is unlike the ordinary claim in the law of torts or delicts that, but for the defendant's negligence, the child would not be handicapped, because, had the defendant exercised due care, a more suitable gamete donor would have been used, and the plaintiff would not have been conceived. That is, the child's claim is that, with due care, another child would have been created by combination of gametes and born in his or her place. The negligence claim may therefore amount to a 'wrongful life' claim, which argues that the plaintiff should not have been born.

A comparable claim may be allowed in some jurisdictions against parents. Legislated or judicially constructed rules of parental immunity may obstruct claims by children,[20] but in principle, as, for instance, in Canadian jurisdictions, it is no bar to proceedings that the relation between plaintiff and defendant is that of child and parent. Accordingly, the issue may arise of whether in selecting a gamete donor, a prospective parent owes a duty of care to the child intended to be conceived and born. A couple may have a legal right to reproduce naturally and risk the birth of a genetically or otherwise congenitally impaired child, but, unless courts are willing to recognize a general right of similarly unrestricted recourse to gamete donation, the same may not hold true for artificial reproduction.

Limits on individual reproductive choice are being contemplated where children born alive would predictably suffer from such conditions as congenital drug addiction and fetal alcohol syndrome. These conditions may be caused *in utero* rather than as genetic consequences of preconception choices of who the gamete donors are to be, however, and may therefore be distinguishable. Complex issues may arise when a child is affected *in utero* or during delivery by the human immunodeficiency virus (HIV) its mother contracted before or after conception, or through a gamete source. These issues may be the same in principle as would arise in natural reproduction, although artificial reproduction opens the possibility of the gamete source supplying not a sperm that leads to conception, but an ovum.

Artificial reproduction through gamete donation may achieve the same family-building results as natural reproduction through legislation, common in the US, that provides that gamete sources outside the family unit, based on a heterosexual union (although some jurisdictions may accommodate same-sex unions *mutatis mutandis*), will have no status regarding a consequently born child. The female member of the unit will be the child's mother for all legal purposes, and the male its father for all legal purposes. His consent to sperm donor assisted reproduction may be presumed unless he records his refusal of consent at or within an appropriate time. Some legislation may alternatively require his prior express consent as a condition of his legal paternity, but this may prejudice a child's status if he subsequently claims to have been deceived in a material particular. Once a child's legal parentage is so determined, such matters as inheritance rights are governed by that determination.

Even in the absence of regularizing legislation, legal presumptions of legitimacy and associated paternity may be tenacious. Almost all legal systems in the Common Law world and many beyond presume that when a married woman gives birth to a child during marriage or within a given time thereafter, usually generously measured, her husband is the father. In most cases of gamete donation, no-one has any incentive to deny this, since all participants intend the husband to be regarded as the father, and the man who supplies the sperm to remain unrecognized. The advent of ovum donation triggers the comparable presumption *mater est quam gestatio demonstrat*,[21] that is that the woman who gestates the child is its mother. It will be seen below that such a presumption may prove dysfunctional regarding surrogate motherhood, and that some opponents have embraced it for that very reason.

A paradox of the reduced significance of children's genetic origins to their settlement within functioning families is the growing significance of knowledge of genetic parentage to medical diagnosis and care, and the improved means of 'genetic fingerprinting' that may identify who a child's genetic parent is. Knowledge of personal characteristics and predispositions of patients is rapidly growing through developments in genetic understanding of parental characteristics. Accordingly, while a gamete donor's identity may be of little or no consequence to a child's psychological and social behaviour, knowledge of the donor's genetic characteristics may be significant to the child's welfare regarding, for instance, diagnosis of sickness and appropriateness of treatment. An obligation may therefore exist ethically and perhaps legally for a health professional managing gamete donation to ensure that non-identifying genetic information about the gamete donor will be available to the subsequently born child, for instance through entry on the child's medical record or through appropriate anonymous linkage. It is not inconceivable, however, that in the future children's means to identify their genetic parents and, when adult, to meet them in person, perhaps by mutual consent, will be available.[22]

Reproduction involving participants in two or more families, whether through serial marriages, unmarried unions or relationships, or artificial means, raises questions about half-siblings of different sexes being or becoming familiar with each other and becoming sexually involved. Inadvertent incest, in which a sexual partner is unaware of the proximate genetic relationship with the other, is not criminally actionable, but may affect the legal status of a marriage entered in good faith when the relationship is subsequently discovered. Even without their knowledge of genetic links between partners in sexual relations who have a common parent, who might have been a gamete donor to a clinic undertaking TDI, the demographic risk of incest is present. Evidence indicates, however, that calculable though dysgenic risks to resulting children are, they are not higher than the incidence of dysgenic risks of ordinary reproduction in populations at large. Accordingly, elaborate and intrusive registration and tracing systems designed to limit inadvertent incest are not warranted. Risk from over-use of a gamete donor to artificial reproduction may be adequately contained by limiting use of an individual donor and distributing each donor's gametes to recipients who live distant from each other.

Family issues in IVF

In so far as donated gametes are used in IVF procedures, they raise the issues of quality control considered above, and may present them in an acute form when a single pregnancy arises in a family when both the ovum and the sperm that combined *in vitro* were donated. There are some special implications of IVF, however, that warrant attention in the setting of the family into which a gestated product of IVF will be born.

The first is familial in the most primal and intimate of ways: the mutual dependency and mutual competition or sibling rivalry presented when multiple production of pre-embryos *in vitro* is followed by multiple implantation and multiple pregnancy. Evidence has produced the widespread IVF practice, when several pre-embryos are created *in vitro*, of implanting three or four. This maximizes the chance of the procedure resulting in continuation of gestation of at least one embryo and fetus, and birth of a single child. A single pre-embryo has less likelihood to complete prenatal life when it enters its gestating mother's uterus alone. Too many pre-embryos and embryos in the same uterus also render it unlikely, however, that any of them will complete gestation, and their cumulative presence endangers the mother's permanent health and very life. The medical response is to advise selective reduction of pregnancy, through a process of abortion that reduces multiple pregnancy to a singleton but usually to a twin or perhaps a triplet pregnancy.

The description of the ultrasonically-guided process of abortion as 'selective' reduction is true numerically, in that the established total of embryos or early fetuses discovered developing in the uterus is reduced to a selected number. Which embryos are targeted for termination is decided, however, not at all selectively. The features or genetic potentials of the embryos are not assessed and the relative qualities of the embryos competing for survival are not sought, as they might be when *in vitro* pre-embryos are chosen for implantation. On the contrary, the choice among embryos may be made arbitrarily and indiscriminately, the most conveniently accessible to the instruments of abortion being taken. The embryos that are terminated are thereby subjected to the sad truth of family membership, that some members may be called upon to bear sacrifices, including the sacrifice of life itself, for others of the family, and that which shall suffer sacrifice and which survive can be decided by the arbitrary forces of fate.

Two further familial problems arising from IVF affect patients of IVF clinics who come to disagree with clinic personnel concerning the destiny and use of their cryopreserved, meaning frozen, pre-embryos, and couples who come to disagree between themselves. Both scenarios have recently been addressed by US trial courts, which reached mutually incompatible findings about the way in which the question of legal status of pre-embryos should be resolved. One or other approach, or neither, may prove correct, and the matter will be determined in time through precedents and persuasive judgements of appellate courts.

The former scenario concerned the celebrated, pioneering IVF programme at the Medical College of Hampton Roads in Norfolk, Virginia.[23] A husband and wife who were patients lived in New Jersey when they were admitted for treatment. Six pre-embryos were created *in vitro*, of which five were implanted, but without success. The sixth pre-embryo was cryopreserved for possible later use, under the terms of a contractual agreement that recognized the couple as legally owning the frozen pre-embryo. The couple moved to California, and about a year after the freezing they asked the Norfolk clinic to send the pre-embryo to an IVF programme in Los Angeles for thawing and attempted implantation. The Virginia programme declined to comply, invoking contractual grounds and the indignity of shipping a human embryo like cattle embryos.

The couple sued for breach of contract, violations of various US Constitutional provisions, and detinue, which is a cause of action for recovery of specific personal property unjustly detained. The clinic filed a motion to dismiss the action. The US federal trial court in Virginia accepted the legal applicability of the property language of the agreement, and interpreted its terms in favour of the couple, permitting their suit to proceed. The court found that the cryopreservation agreement created a bailment relationship which imposed on the clinic, as bailee, an obligation to return the subject matter of the bailment to the bailor, that is the couple, or to dispatch it at their direction.

This decision of July, 1989 was not followed in September 1989 by a County Circuit Court of Tennessee in the *Davis* case.[24] In an unprecedented decision, the trial judge adopted an approach that the large majority of respected commentators doubted would be upheld on appeal, when, describing frozen pre-embryos[25] as 'human beings existing as embryos' and 'children *in vitro*', he applied principles of child custody law. The judge might have reached the same outcome of the case on other, more conventional grounds, so the actual decision might have survived appeal, but its reasoning was highly suspect.

The case arose when a couple, whose seven frozen pre-embryos were held by an IVF clinic, separated. The wife, fearing that they represented her last chance to bear her own child, wanted to ensure that the pre-embryos would be available to her in the future for thawing and attempted implantation. The husband opposed this prospect on the ground that he did not want control of whether he would become a father to be in the sole hands of his separated, and, as she became his divorced, wife. Finding that the pre-embryos were not simply analogous to children, but were already 'children *in vitro*', the judge applied child custody principles, which centre on protection and advancement of children's best interests. Mrs Davis's claim of entitlement to control the pre-embryos was upheld not because her claim to them was stronger than that of her husband's, but because it was compatible with the interests of the pre-embryos themselves. The judge did not address the fact that if an embryo was to become successfully implanted in Mrs Davis, she would be legally entitled to an abortion without regard to the best interests of the embryo.

The claim of Mrs Davis might have succeeded on several alternative grounds. The court might have found it an implied term of the cryopreservation agreement between the couple that Mrs Davis could seek implantation without her husband's agreement through her control of property held in common. It might also have been found that, in the same way as a husband surrenders control of whether he becomes a father to his wife following natural insemination, Mr Davis yielded that control after *in vitro* insemination. Mrs Davis's claim might additionally have been favoured because, while her husband could not compel the introduction of the pre-embryos into her uterus involuntarily, her wish for implantation was not dependent on any bodily invasion of him or action by him, and that her initiative to employ the pre-embryos should be favoured over his preference that they be wasted. The *Davis* decision might satisfactorily have been based on the comparable outcome reached by a French court regarding posthumous use of frozen semen in the *Parpalaix* case.[26]

The policy preference that the case clearly reinforces, which is in fact now followed by almost all IVF clinics in North America, is that couples who enter IVF programmes that include cryopreservation of pre-embryos should say in advance how they are to be managed under such future possibilities as the death of either or both of them, and their divorce, separation or disagreement on disposition. IVF clinics may introduce conditions on which they are prepared to collaborate which may include a dispute resolving formula or the choice of options the clinic is prepared to accommodate, with a predetermined residual disposition in the absence of any positive agreement otherwise. In countries such as the UK, legislation such as a Human Fertilisation and Embryology Act will be applicable to set limits, for instance, on storage and on disposition of pre-embryos.

The judge in the *Davis* case appears not to have considered the trapdoor he opened beneath his own ideology, which strongly incorporated the language and values of the conservative Pro Life or anti-abortion movement.[27] Adherents of this movement are not necessarily confined to or composed exclusively of a religiously-based core, but are generally inclined to be sympathetic to positions expressed in particular by Roman Catholic religious leaders, who oppose reproductive techniques that depart from a conservatively perceived sense of what is 'natural'. To this sense, surrogate motherhood is objectionable, and more so when a pre-embryo that originated in IVF is implanted in a gestational or carrying mother.[28] The Tennessee judge referred approvingly to the New Jersey *Baby* M case that strongly disapproved of SM,[29] but failed to follow the logic of his own convictions.

If a court in a custody case involving a pre-embryo is committed exclusively to serving its best interests, the court might still decline to order at the request of the biological father that it be placed in the uterus of the biological mother over her objection, but presumably would approve its placement in the uterus of a different, willing woman despite the biological mother's objection. That is, had Mr Davis found a willing surrogate, the court would have allowed the pre-embryo to be placed in her over objection by Mrs Davis, because it would be in the best interests of the pre-embryo to have this sole prospect of development rather than be wasted through non-implantation. The same would have been the case had Mrs Davis wanted to engage a surrogate mother rather than to gestate a pre-embryo herself over Mr Davis's objection, and had either Mr or Mrs Davis been prepared to pay for the SM service. The policy objection that such a transaction might be exploitive of the volunteer gestating mother could not prevail over the pre-embryonic 'child's' best interests because, as the judge observed, in custody cases the law 'turns its full focus on the best interests of the child; its concern is not for those who claim "rights" to the child, nor for those who claim custody of the child, nor for those who may suffer perceived or real inequities resulting from [the law's] scrupiously (sic) guarding the child's best interests.'[30] Accordingly, if gestation through commercially procured SM serves a pre-embryonic best interest better than wastage and oblivion, the *Davis* trial judgement would afford such an arrangement acceptance and enforcement. Its unconscious but implicit accommodation of SM is not the reason, however, or the only reason, why the rationalization in the case is better considered incorrect.

Following divorce, Mrs Davis remarried and, not wanting a child in her new relationship, decided to donate the pre-embryos under her control to infertile couples for implantation. The Tennessee Court of Appeal subsequently set aside the trial court's decision and ordered that the pre-embryos be under the joint control of Mr Davis and the former Mrs Davis.

Family issues in Surrogate Motherhood

It has been seen above that SM can be either partial SM or, with technological assistance of IVF or embryo recovery following *in vivo* fertilization, 'full' or 'total' SM in which the gestating mother is not genetically related to the embryo/fetus she bears. It has also been seen that under the legal presumption that a woman who gestates a child is its mother for all legal purposes to the exclusion of others (*mater est quam gestatio demonstrat*),[31] which helpfully achieves the goals of ovum donation, SM is frustrated. This is the purpose, for instance, of the UK Human Fertilisation and Embryology Bill, which provides in clause 26(1) that 'A woman who has carried a child as a result of the placing in her of an embryo or of sperm and eggs, and no other woman, is to be treated as the mother of the child.'[32] Use of the past tense 'has carried' and the term 'a child', rather than of the present tense 'carries' and of the term 'an embryo' and/or 'a fetus' leaves open the issue of whether such motherhood commences at delivery and whether another woman may be recognized as 'mother' while the embryo/fetus is *in utero*. While it is *in vitro* awaiting placement in a prospective surrogate mother, it may be premature to describe her as its mother, although after birth, and arguably during its gestation *in vivo*, she will be its mother according to provisions of the Bill.

The Bill also makes explicit what in any event is probably implicit under general provisions of most legal systems, namely that 'No surrogacy arrangement is enforceable by or against any of the persons making it.'³³ Unenforceability of agreements does not in itself make them unlawful; indeed many contracts for performance of personal services are not specifically enforceable through the courts but nevertheless lawful. Voluntary compliance produces consequences the law recognizes, and refusal or failure to comply may be legally compensated, but not by an order to perform an activity. Contracts for SM may be held void as contrary to public policy, however, because of ideological hostility to the commerce and commodification of children perceived to arise from paid SM.

Such a provision may indeed be dysfunctional to serve the goal of reducing the profit motive in SM. The *Baby M* case tended to reinforce an ideological conviction that SM recruits and exploits primarily low-income women, and satisfies wealthy people at the emotional and physical expense of a socio-economic and educational sub-class of women, which in a proportion of unregulated instances of SM may be so. As against this, however, a small number of anecdotes have emerged in the US of surrogate mothers declining to surrender the children they have delivered, not because of emotional or psychological bonding to them, but because they want a higher payment than was originally arranged. Unenforceability of the agreements has empowered them to impose conditions of increased payment that, even if they are unlawful as in breach for instance of adoption legislation, the commissioning parents who pay have a strong incentive to suppress and deny. Unenforceability may therefore facilitate ransom, baby selling and the unconscionable commerce and commodification it is invoked to prevent.

The unavailability of paid SM services, and of paid brokers to arrange such services, to create a 'new' family can exert strains on a conventional family where it is realized that SM is feasible.³⁴ An infertile couple, or one in which the wife suffers chronic spontaneous abortion or a condition such as a cardiac disease that makes gestation impossible or a grave danger, may be dependent on another woman for any prospect of having a child of at least one of them. If they cannot employ services to find a woman outside the circle of family and close friends, a suitable potential surrogate mother within that circle may feel immense pressure to agree to serve. Pressure may come, or be sensed, not only from the couple but from other family members, such as those whose prospects of grandparenthood and continuation of a family line and name depend on SM. A refusal to serve may become a source of resentment, friction and continuing disharmony and eventually division among the circle of family or friends. The couple may blame the reluctant potential surrogate mother for their childlessness, and the eligible woman may feel resentment at the pressure if she does not yield to it, and if she does.

Legal prohibition of commercial SM and brokers may protect women against exploitation of their low economic status and prospects, but its enactment will not necessarily protect women against pressures arising from friendships and family membership. Further, a child surrendered in a SM arrangement to social parents who are related to the gestating mother, who will itself have a continuing relationship with her, may experience role confusion. The child may be uncertain whether to relate to her as, for instance, her niece or nephew, second cousin, grandchild, or child. Being gestated by a stranger to its social family may be in the child's best interests, although perhaps too much should not be made of this speculative disadvantage.[35]

Prohibition of SM is not the only legal response to fears of social and personal harm from such arrangements. As an exercise in damage control designed neither to ban SM nor to facilitate it, but to regulate it in the interests of prospective participants and particularly children who will in fact be born and surrendered in conformity with such arrangements, whether paid or unpaid, the Ontario Law Reform Commission has proposed that family courts be able to hear applications for prior judicial approval.[36] Judges in so-called Surrogate Adoption cases would hear what parties have privately arranged, and decide whether it can receive judicial approval consistently with legislated criteria and those developed by experience and through past judgements. Even in the absence of legislation approving the proposal, an Ontario court has followed the recorded practice of a Michigan court[37] in specifying that, in the case of full SM, births of the twin children in issue were to be registered in the name of the genetic/commissioning mother, and not of the gestating mother. This compresses the process of routine birth registration followed by adoption proceedings in which that registration is ordered sealed from inspection and a new birth certificate is issued showing the name only of the commissioning mother.

Whether or not SM is preceded or followed by judicial adoption or quasi-adoption proceedings, it has a true potential to create family relations that are not only new, but previously unimagined. An early case in South Africa saw a woman gestate her own daughter's embryo, her genetic grandchild. Cryopreservation in IVF may permit comparable generational confusion if preservation and thawing techniques improve. For instance, one of two embryos conceived *in vitro* at the same time may be gestated and grow up as a young woman in whose uterus the second is then implanted. The main obstacle to such an occurrence may be finding a reason why anyone would want to undertake it, unless for instance to initiate and terminate a pregnancy in order to procure genetically compatible fetal tissues for transplantation. More understandable may be a woman's willingness to offer SM to an embryo of her immediately pre-menopausal step-mother and father, or of her sister-in-law and brother. No incest would arise in law or genetics, of course, in such full SM.

Permutations of interactions among gamete sources and gestating mothers may be limited principally by human imagination, ingenuity, responses to desperation and tolerance. At a time when the deliberate founding of single-parent families may still appear unorthodox, our reproductive technologies may seem already to have outstripped our comfortable acceptance of domestic innovation, and to pose a challenge to tolerance that our more conservative institutions and ideologies may need time to meet.

Notes

1. See Bainham, 'When is a Parent not a Parent? Reflections on the Unmarried Father and his Child in English Law' 3 *Int'l J of Law and the Family* (1989), pp. 208–239.
2. Private records are also often Church-related, notably family bibles.
3. See Glendon, *The New Family and the New Property* Toronto: Butterworths, 1981.
4. See Bumpass and Sweet, 'Children's Experience in Single-Parent Families: Implications of Cohabitation and Marital Transitions' 21 *Family Planning Perspectives* (1989), pp. 256–265.
5. *Id*.
6. See e.g., Corea, *The Mother Machine: Reproductive Technologies from Artificial Insemination to Artificial Wombs* New York: Harper and Row, 1985; Corea, Duelli Klein et al. (eds.), *Man-Made Women: How New Reproductive Technologies Affect Women* London: Hutchinson, 1985.
7. Which might include so-called 'chemical pregnancies', identified by measurements of the body's preparation for pregnancy, which may be in vain.
8. See note 6, *supra*.
9. See Congress of the United States, Office of Technology Assessment *Infertility: Medical and Social Choices* Washington D.C.: U.S. Government Printing Office, 1988.

10. See Population Information Program, Johns Hopkins University *Population Reports*, Series L No. 4 (1983).
11. See Cook and Dickens, 'A Decade of International Change in Abortion Law: 1967-1977' 68 *Amer. J. Public Health* (1978), pp. 637-644; and *id*. 'International Developments in Abortion Laws: 1977-1988' 78 *Amer. J. Public Health* (1988), pp. 1305–1311.
12. The observation made by Professor Gregory Baum in his address 'A Roman Catholic Perspective' given on the Panel Session *Preventing HIV Transmission: Religious Conflicts in Public Health?*, at the Fifth International Conference on AIDS, June 7, 1989, Montreal, Canada.
13. Congregation for the Doctrine of the Faith, *Instruction on Respect for Human Life in its Origin and on the Dignity of Proceation* (Vatican City, 1987), p. 37.
14. See note 9, *supra*.
15. See *In re Adoption Application (Payment for Adoption)*, [1987] 3 W.L.R. 31 (Fam. Div.).
16. *In re Baby M* 525 A. 2d 1128 (1987).
17. See the explanation of psychological parenthood in Goldstein, Freud and Solnit, *Beyond the Best Interests of the Child* New York: The Free Press, 1979.
18. See Ernst, 'Psychological Aspects of Artificial Procreation' 3 *International Journal of Law and the Family* (1989), pp. 89–105.
19. See Dickens, 'Wrongful Birth and Life, Wrongful Death Before Birth, and Wrongful Law' in McLean (ed.) *Legal Issues in Human Reproduction* London: Gower Medico-Legal Series, 1989, pp. 80–112.
20. See Mason and McCall Smith, *Law and Medical Ethics* London, Butterworths, 2nd ed. 1987 94 *et seq*.
21. *Id*. at 57.
22. The pattern for this may be developments in adoption law. Sweden, for instance, permits adult children of artificial reproduction to discover their genetic parents' identities.
23. *York v. Jones* 717 F. Supp. 421 (1989).
24. *Davis v. Davis* 15 FLR 2097 (1989).
25. The judge declined to recognize the biologically used word 'pre-embryo', finding no difference in law between a pre-embryo and an embryo. In *York v. Jones*, note 23 above, the judge spoke throughout of a 'pre-zygote'.
26. See Jones, 'Artificial Procreation, Societal Reconceptions: Legal Insight from France' 36 *Amer. J. Comparative Law* (1988), pp. 525–545.
27. See Dickens, 'Abortion and Distortion of Justice in the Law' 17 *Law, Medicine and Health Care* (1989), pp. 395–406.
28. See note 13, *supra*.
29. See note 16, *supra*.
30. Note 24, *supra* at 2104.

31. See note 21, *supra*.
32. Clause 26(2) provides an exception for adoption.
33. Clause 32(1), which amends the Surrogacy Arrangements Act 1985 by insertion of a new section 1A.
34. See Andrews, *New Conceptions: A Consumer's Guide to the Newest Infertility Treatments* New York: St. Martin's Press, 1984, p. 203.
35. See note 18, *supra*.
36. Ontario Law Reform Commission, *Report on Human Artificial Reproduction and Related Matters* (2 vols.) Toronto: Ministry of the Attorney General, 1985.
37. *Smith* v. *Jones*, Circuit Court, County of Wayne, Michigan, No. 85-532014-62 (1986).

3. Patients, families and genetic information
Ian M. Pullen

>I am the family face;
>Flesh perishes, I live on.
>>*Thomas Hardy, 'Heredity'*

Over the past few decades, improvements in living standards and advances in medicine have led to a gradual decline in the incidence of nutritional deficiencies and infectious diseases in childhood. As these conditions have declined, others have been uncovered which are largely, or even entirely, genetically determined.

Many common disorders have a genetic component but are not entirely genetically determined, environmental factors playing some part. These conditions are referred to as being multifactorial. They include common congenital malformations (such as spina bifida, cleft lip and palate), certain diseases associated with modern society (coronary artery disease, diabetes), various major psychiatric disorders (schizophrenia, manic-depressive psychosis) and probably many common cancers. In most multifactorial disorders, the risk to relatives is low (less than one in twenty) and some are treatable. For some, at least, it is possible to reduce the risks by modifying the significant environmental factors. Those with a family history of lung cancer should refrain from smoking. The relapse rate for schizophrenia may be reduced by lowering emotional tension in the home.

Other disorders are entirely genetically determined, environmental factors playing no part. These include single gene (unifactorial) disorders such as Huntington's disease and Duchenne muscular dystrophy, and various abnormalities of chromosome number or structure (cytogenetic abnormalities such as Down's syndrome). Over 3000 unifactorial, and more than 50 cytogenetic disorders have been recognized. While most of these are rare, within an affected family the risk to relatives is high (up to one in two). The disorders are serious and very few are treatable. Because the environment plays no part, manipulation of environmental factors has no effect. Families at risk of these disorders face considerable stress and are required to make very difficult decisions. It is in this situation that genetic counselling has an important role to play.[1]

In the last few years prenatal diagnosis has been a major

development which has removed much of the uncertainty about genetic counselling. Amniocentesis is the technique by which a small quantity of amniotic fluid is withdrawn via a needle passed through the abdominal wall of the mother. The biochemistry of the fluid can be studied to exclude such conditions as spina bifida or anencephaly. The cells in the fluid can be cultured and examined for various chromosome abnormalities, such as Down's syndrome and biochemical studies, including inborn errors of metabolism. The sex of the fetus can be determined if the mother is at risk of having a son with a serious X-linked disorder which is manifested only in males. Amniocentesis is associated with a one to two per cent increased risk of spontaneous abortion.[2]

Amniocentesis is usually performed at about sixteen weeks gestation and cannot be carried out much before fourteen weeks. This means for any diagnosis requiring cell culture, the results will not be available before the pregnancy has progressed to twenty weeks or more. By this stage the mother should have felt fetal movements and termination of pregnancy will be a much more psychologically traumatic option.

The technique of chorion biopsy has been introduced recently. As early as ten weeks of gestation, a cannula is inserted through the cervix into the uterine cavity to permit biopsy of the chorionic villi which are of fetal origin. These cells can be used for some tests immediately without the need for culture, thus saving several weeks. Chorion biopsy can be carried out much earlier than amniocentesis so that, where indicated, earlier termination is possible. But this technique is associated with a higher loss of pregnancy, because around ten per cent of pregnancies abort spontaneously at this stage of pregnancy anyway.

The most recent development involves recombinant DNA technology, more popularly known as genetic engineering. The double helical structure of DNA was discovered in 1953, but it was not until the 1970s that molecular biology really took off with the advent of recombinant DNA techniques. Restriction enzymes have the property of breaking DNA molecules at specific locations (restriction sites) defined by a specific sequence of DNA molecules to produce a lot of small pieces of DNA. If the restriction site is quite close to a particular gene, then it will almost certainly be inherited with it. If the gene is absent, then the restriction site is missing and the usual break will not occur, leaving a longer piece of unbroken DNA. This difference can be detected. Thus it is not necessary to know precisely where the gene is on the chromosome or to be able to test for it directly to be able to predict with considerable accuracy whether or not the gene has been inherited. All it requires is to be able to use a restriction site that is known to be close to the gene and will therefore act as a marker for it. This technique has been used to diagnoze such conditions as cystic fibrosis, Duchenne muscular dystrophy and Huntington's disease.

The recent development of new genetic techniques has widened the scope for diagnostic and predictive testing for a wide range of inherited conditions. Yet the discovery of such a condition has far reaching implications for the family concerned and raises profound psychological, ethical, social and legal issues. Recognition of these issues, and a better understanding of normal coping processes and counselling techniques, has changed the emphasis in genetic counselling. The genetic counsellor's role has shifted away from that of educator and instructor, to information-giver and person-orientated counsellor.[3]

Problems in genetic counselling

A number of key issues confront the family, geneticist and society in connection with the genetic counselling process. What, at first sight might seem to be a simple enough transaction, is beset with ethical and legal problems. An individual or couple seek help, a detailed family tree is constructed, tests are conducted on the counsellee(s) and medical information is requested on key family members, who may also be examined or tested. A diagnosis is made, risks of inheritance are calculated, options discussed and decisions made. These may include undertaking a therapeutic abortion, sterilization, artificial insemination by donor (AID), or deciding to do nothing.

An initial question is whether everyone has a right of access to this counselling and testing process? Certainly services should be available to those individuals who are capable of participating in the process and understanding the significance of the findings and the options open to them. Having excluded the severely mentally impaired (demented and severely mentally handicapped), should there be a restriction on the basis of age? It would seem sensible to offer open access to those over the age of majority (eighteen). But what about the sixteen-year-old contemplating marriage who wants to determine the risk of having an affected child, or the thirteen-year-old girl who discovers that she is pregnant? Maturity is a better guide but difficult to legislate for.

If individuals have a right to counselling and testing if they so wish, then in a free society they must also have the right to decide not to participate. Returning to the under age pregnant girl; what rights does she have if her mother (her legal guardian) demands that she (or her fetus) be tested? Vulnerable individuals must be protected from undue pressure to submit to a process that they would wish to avoid. Most vulnerable of all is the baby offered for adoption. Testing of his genetic status might blight his prospects for adoption and a normal family life.

The newer genetic tests all rely on the genetic material derived from blood, fluid or cell samples. The DNA derived from these materials may be deep frozen and stored indefinitely. This process itself gives rise to a host of problems. Who owns this genetic material; the donor or the laboratory? Once donated, does the laboratory have the right to use the samples for research, to help with the diagnosis of other family members, or to subject the sample to other tests? One group insists that the legal ownership of stored DNA remains with the depositor,[4] but practice varies from service to service. It would seem good practice to make clear, in writing, the basis on which blood is being donated, and to collect a fresh sample or request a change of use before other tests are performed.

If the ownership of the sample is contentious, then the ownership of any test result is doubly so. Here the most pressing matter is that of who has a right to that highly sensitive information and what measures should be taken to safeguard its confidentiality. The donor of the sample has an inalienable right to the result, but it is not clear whether such a right extends to anybody else. What about his general practitioner (GP) who is, at least in Britain, responsible for his everyday medical care? GPs may be approached by employers or insurance companies and are obliged, with the patient's consent, to provide relevant results. If the GP is not informed of test results, this will at least protect the patient, but may be to his disadvantage. It may be critically important for children to know the diagnosis of a deteriorating parent, or for a spouse or prospective spouse to have this information, but this is not to say that they have a right to it. However appropriate a request for such information may seem, confidentiality cannot be broken except with the individual's permission.

Many couples will have to face the painful decision as to whether or not to seek an abortion. For some, this will be totally unacceptable on religious or moral grounds. For others, the dilemma will centre on the criteria for taking such a decision. There are many factors to be taken into account, including the quality of life for the future child, for the family, and, of course, for future generations. How severe a condition should trigger this response, and what about conditions that only manifest themselves much later in life? These must remain choices to be taken by those who will have to live with the consequences of their decision.

A two year follow-up study of 200 consecutive couples seen in an Edinburgh genetic counselling clinic demonstrated the gap between the counsellor's expectations and the actual consequences of counselling.[5] Over a third of those who were told that they were at high risk of having a child with a serious genetic disease were undeterred and actually planned further pregnancies. When the couples were carefully questioned, their decisions were often very understandable. For example, further pregnancies were planned in some cases because, after seeing the effects of a disorder in a previous child or in one of the parents, it was not considered sufficiently serious, or prenatal diagnosis was available, or if a subsequent child was affected it would not survive. There was also a small but lamentable group of couples who had no living children and dearly wanted a family at whatever cost.

Finally, in addition to the requirement to act responsibly and safeguard specimens and results, there is a need for genetic counselling services to ensure that those seeking help are given appropriate support after the results have been communicated. Coming to terms with the information that they have been given takes time, and for many will be helped by outside support. Those developing new tests must take ethical considerations into account. Is it ethical to offer to detect whether an individual has inherited an untreatable condition that might not appear for several decades, or should research be directed first at treatment?

The counselling process

Genetic counselling is essentially a process of communication between the counsellor and those who seek genetic counselling. There are three situations that frequently lead to the request for counselling. A couple who have had an abnormal child may come to learn what has gone wrong and discover the risk of recurrence in a future pregnancy. A couple with a family history of genetic disorder may wish to determine the risk of having an affected child before embarking on pregnancy. During pregnancy they may wish to check the genetic status of the fetus before deciding whether to continue with the pregnancy. To this list must now be added the newest presymptomatic testing. Individuals with a family history of a disorder that might only manifest itself in later life may wish to discover whether or not they have inherited the gene.

The first and most important task is to confirm the diagnosis. This begins with the construction of an extensive family tree recording who has been affected by what condition. This must then be double checked. This may involve tracing the medical records of deceased relatives and contacting the doctors of affected living relatives, as well as examining and investigating members of the immediate family. Without this painstaking and thorough assessment no valid counselling can take place.

The information to be communicated in the genetics clinic falls roughly into three main areas. First, information about the disorder itself. This includes severity and prognosis, and whether or not there is any effective treatment; what the genetic mechanism is that caused the disease and what are the risks of it recurring in the family. Second, information on the available options open to a couple who find that the risk of having an affected child is unacceptably high. These options may include contraception (including sterilization), adoption, artificial insemination by donor (AID), and prenatal diagnosis with selective abortion. Third, and most recent, has been the question of detecting the likelihood of the individual having inherited a condition which has yet to manifest itself (pre-symptomatic testing).

There are very serious problems in attempting to communicate information of such a personal and delicate nature in a situation where parents may be grieving over the loss of an abnormal child, or coping with the realization that they are at risk of passing on the condition to their future offspring. They may feel shell-shocked, bedevilled by feelings of guilt, and suffer a profound loss of self esteem and any sense of purpose in their life. They may be overwhelmed by feelings of anger at God for the apparent injustice of their position, and be extremely hostile to relatives who might have been guilty of concealing the family history. In addition, information about genetic conditions is rarely emotionally neutral and often has profound psychological effects.

Before analyzing the specific psychological reactions encountered in sufferers and their families, the 'normal' reaction to adversity should be considered. It has been proposed that we all function in a state of emotional equilibrium which is a dynamic process. Any perceived threat upsets this steady state causing a rise in tension and provoking a sequence of coping manoeuvres aimed at restoring equilibrium.[6] Although the specific reaction will be dictated by circumstances and the individual's personality, most reactions will follow a similar sequence of stages. The most extensively studied such reaction is normal grief following bereavement. Most people will experience a brief period of numbness and disbelief before progressing to the full grief reaction including guilt, anger, depression, loss of appetite, poor sleep, ruminations about what has happened, and how it might have been prevented. Finally, in due time, the relationship with the dead person is set in perspective, some psychological separation is made, and the individual is free to begin to take up his life and make new plans and new relationships.

Man has only a limited repertoire of coping manoeuvres. Most setbacks in life will spark off a coping process very similar to the grief reaction. In the case of inherited disorders there will be a marked reaction to the discovery that there is an illness in the family and that members are at risk. There will be grief for the loss of normality and the threat of illness. If the condition is autosomal recessive (inherited equally from both parent) both parents 'share the blame' equally. An X-linked (sex linked) disease places particular strain on asymptomatic female carriers of the disease. An autosomal dominant illness (inherited from only one parent) puts all the 'blame' on one parent. If the illness is of late onset, the relationship between parent and child is quite different. The still normal child witnesses in the parent what he or she may become. If there is an early diagnostic test, the child knows the fate to expect. The child lives in a situation in which the affected parent is like a living mirror of the child's own future.[7]

Huntington's disease

Huntington's disease (HD) was first described in 1872. It is an autosomal dominant late onset disorder that affects about 1 in 10000 of the general population. So there are about 6000 sufferers in the UK and a further 50000 at risk. There are some parts of the country with much higher rates (especially East Anglia, and parts of Scotland and South Wales).[8] Each child of a parent with HD has a fifty per cent chance of inheriting the condition. The usual age of onset is in the third or fourth decade, which means that a couple may well have completed their family before the condition appears. They then have to cope with the illness in one generation while continuing to worry about which of their children has inherited the gene. There is no effective treatment. Individuals watch themselves, watch their siblings, watch their parents, watch their children.[7]

HD affects almost every aspect of functioning. The body gradually becomes taken over by involuntary movements which are continuous throughout waking and sleeping hours alike. Mood is altered, usually becoming depressed, sometimes to the point of suicide. Thinking, reasoning and planning become disrupted, judgement goes awry and memory is impaired. Speech is lost, self care is impossible, choking is frequent and death may be a welcome relief.[7]

The problem has been the lack of any way of predicting who has inherited the gene and who has not. An individual who has inherited the gene will pass it on to half his or her children, who in turn will pass it on to half of their children, whereas the individual who has not inherited the gene cannot pass it on to future generations. Not only will he or she have normal children, but they in turn will have normal offspring. This very real risk of having affected children and perpetuating the disease in the family led to the advice, in the past, for those at risk not to have children. In the 1970s an attempt was made to use L-dopa as a predictive test. It was thought that those who had inherited the gene would develop abnormal involuntary movements when exposed to the drug. The reliability of this distressing test was soon questioned, and it was quickly discontinued.[9]

In 1983 Guesella and colleagues published in *Nature* the discovery of a polymorphic DNA marker genetically linked to HD.[10] They had studied one very large Venezuelan family living on the shores of Lake Maracaibo, the descendents of one German sailor who is thought to have gone ashore while his ship was berthed in the local harbour. Using restriction enzymes (gene probes) they were fortunate enough to find DNA fragments from the DNA of sufferers and their relatives with the same sort of frequency as would be expected, that is, it was inherited in the same pattern as the HD gene. This fragment of DNA from chromosome 4 is not the gene itself (it is too large) but is close to it and serves as a marker for HD. There is a small chance of the DNA recombining which may produce false positive or false negative results, making the reliability of the test up to ninety-eight per cent. This, of course, is not a test of the gene itself (unlike with cystic fibrosis or Duchenne muscular dystrophy), but the detection of a pattern of inheritance by inference, and therefore it involves other members of the family. In fact, more than one generation is required to co-operate, including family members who are affected and those who are unaffected and old enough to be at risk. In this way this form of testing is quite different from any former investigation and raises major psychological, ethical and legal questions.

The diagnosis of Huntington's disease sends shock waves through a family. The period of numbness and disbelief is soon replaced by the full reaction. Who knew of this disease in the family? Who has been hiding the knowledge? Who is to blame? Which family, which individuals? How on earth can this news be true? How can we cope? Have I got it? Am I going to suffer from uncontrollable movements, lose my memory, dement, become aggressive and totally dependent before choking to death in some impersonal institution? If I've not inherited it then my sister must have done – it's almost as though I have given it to her.

Anger, despair, depression, anxiety and guilt are 'normal' reactions. With time, a supportive family, the help of friends and where necessary, counselling, resolution comes. The hurt and uncertainty remains with life taking on the appearance of Russian roulette.[7] Self-monitoring for early signs of unsteadiness or clumsiness becomes automatic, but life goes on. The individual is not totally overwhelmed by these thoughts and plans are made to continue with education, take a holiday, get married and think about having children. But some people do become casualties. The initial stress sometimes precipitates a major psychiatric illness (usually a major depressive illness) requiring specific treatment. Alcohol and drugs may be used to blot out the distress and bring temporary relief. Feelings of anger may lead to violence towards others or attacks on property. Parasuicide (self injury) may be followed by suicide.

The family with an affected member tends to become isolated. The affected person may wish to hide, or may be hidden away. The secrecy and guilt may lead to a communal sense of failure. The family may be stigmatized and avoided by others. This will have a direct effect on the normal development of children. Memory disturbance, bizarre behaviour, violence and incontinence make the home a place to be avoided. In some cases, of course, this bleak picture is absent. There are many families who cope admirably with what seems to others to be an intolerable situation. They care for the affected person with great love and frequently with surprising humour.

All of this will have an impact on genetic counselling. The process of information giving and receiving is severely impaired by many of the reactions experienced in the normal coping process. Anxiety and poor concentration hamper memory registration. Anger and guilt make the counselling relationship difficult. Psychiatric illness may render the individual inaccessible for a time. It is therefore essential to assess which stage of the coping process has been reached by each counsellee.[6]

The genetic counselling process itself is stressful. The initial session will concentrate on the family tree. It will bring to the fore old family skeletons long hidden from sight. It will draw attention to the number of people in the family who have developed and died of the condition. But perhaps most threatening of all, it might include a physical examination and other investigations to establish whether or not the individual is manifesting signs of the disease. Later in the sessions the question of antenatal testing, termination of pregnancy and pre-symptomatic testing will be raised. Each of these carries its own ethical, moral and psychological elements. One question, in particular, that needs to be asked, but often avoided, concerns suicidal thoughts and plans. This will be considered further in connection with presymptomatic testing.

For some years geneticists and self-help groups such as the Huntington's Chorea Association and Combat have debated the principle of pre-symptomatic and antenatal testing. Surely any test that can remove the Sword of Damocles from above the heads of fifty per cent of those at risk must be a good thing? But what about the other fifty per cent, those who have all hope of having avoided the gene taken away? Some argued that presymptomatic testing should not be developed before some form of treatment was available, and the search for a treatment should be the research priority. Even when the technique had been developed, perhaps it should only be used for antenatal testing.

It has to be remembered that the new recombinant DNA test for Huntington's disease does not detect the gene itself, but infers the presence or absence of the gene from the size of the DNA fragments produced when DNA is in the presence of a particular enzyme. To make sense of these results, DNA from more than one generation of family members, both affected and unaffected have to be tested. The involvement of other family members not only makes the test much more complicated to perform, but raises many additional ethical and psychological issues. Unfortunately not all families will be informative. Unless more than one generation is available for testing, including affected and clearly unaffected (older) members, the test is not possible. It is estimated that the test will be possible in only forty per cent of cases.

Why test in the first place? If the test is negative (a very high probability that the gene has not been inherited) that individual can plan for the future without regard to the likelihood of developing the illness in middle age or having affected children. Above all the stress of living under threat will be removed, enhancing the quality of life for the individual and his immediate family. If the test is 'positive' (a very high probability that the gene has been inherited) some of the uncertainty is removed. It is highly probable that the condition will develop, but the test gives no indication as to when that might happen. The individual might decide to bring forward certain plans to ensure that they are completed while he or she is still fit. Other plans may be abandoned, such as a decision to work abroad. Housing can be planned with the need for ground floor accommodation being taken into account. The question of children can be addressed in the clear knowledge of the genetic status of one parent. The couple may decide to have children early to improve the chance of the children being relatively independent by the time the illness strikes. They may decide to avoid having a family because of the risk to their children. They may want to consider antenatal testing with the hope of maximizing their chance of having children who will not be at risk of Huntington's.

If the test is inconclusive, as will sometimes happen, the individual is left with the same uncertainty, a fifty per cent chance of having inherited the gene. But at least he or she will know that they have tried to determine their status, not just for themselves, but for the next generation. Thus the mechanics of the test requires family cooperation. The social, ethical and moral issues have been clearly debated by Smurl, Weaver and Lamport.[11,12] Their papers provide the basis for much of the following.

Some of those required to give blood, and to be examined for the presence or absence of the illness, might never have met or even have heard of the family member requesting the test. They may have a moral duty to do what they can for another human being, particularly someone to whom they are related, but their involvement will also throw up information about themselves. What happens if it is clear to the examining doctor that they are manifesting the early signs of the condition? They have not asked for that information. What happens to the result of the test on their DNA? Do they have a right to know the result? Can they be sure of the confidentiality regarding their sample?

What happens if someone refuses to co-operate? Can someone be forced to give blood? Certainly not at present, but there are precedents for compelling someone to provide a sample in the case of murder enquiries, drunk driving charges and some paternity suits. While the law does not apply to predictive testing, what protection is there for relatives who do not wish to be involved. In particular, there is the issue of protecting those who are especially vulnerable because of their youth or because of intellectual impairment as a result of being affected, from undue pressure. Participation will give indirect information about the status of some members of the family. A 'positive result' confirms that the parent must have inherited and passed on the gene. Thus the parent, without having requested testing, or, importantly, without receiving pre-test counselling, may be confronted with his or her own status without appropriate preparation or support.

Who has a right to genetic information? The simple rule of thumb operated by most departments of clinical genetics is as follows. Information given by an individual seeking genetic counselling is privileged medical information that must be treated with strict confidentiality. The storage must be secure and details may only be disclosed to the counsellee's general medical practitioner or another doctor with the consent of the counsellee. Nobody else should have access to that information. However, in Britain medical case records are frequently sub poena'd by the courts in cases of divorce. They are then open to inspection by the lawyers for another party, and may be seen by other family members.

Quite apart from the mechanics for securing and maintaining confidentiality, there is the question of the rights of others to knowledge about an individual's genetic status. Does a child have the right to have information about his parents; does a spouse have the right to knowledge before making decisions about pregnancy; does a child have a right to know that he has not inherited the gene? What about the rights of others or organizations unrelated to the individual? Do employers have a right to know about the genetic status of an employee, especially if that employee is in a very responsible post? Should they know if a train driver, airline pilot, air traffic controller, surgeon or financial director has inherited the gene which will affect, at some stage, his judgement and intellect? In the case of insurance companies, do they have the right to information that will alter the risk they are insuring, and do they or employers have the right to insist that a test is taken? In this case, what would be the right of the relatives who would have to co-operate?

Smurl and Weaver have drawn attention to the guidelines produced in the USA for research and clinical practice in the area of Huntington's disease.[11] They consider that these are based on the general moral and legal principles of autonomy, informed consent, beneficence, truth-telling and promise-keeping. They point out that this is a unique experience in that there has been no previous similar test. Not only does it require this degree of family co-operation, but it results in information about an illness that might not manifest itself for a further twenty or thirty years and for which there is no treatment.

Specific problems: abortion and suicide

It was expected that when first introduced the test would be used for prenatal exclusion rather than the presymptomatic testing of adults. This would perhaps avoid some of these ethical problems. Antenatal testing requires the same range of co-operative adults from different generations including both affected and unaffected individuals. The testing of all these samples to establish the inheritance pattern within the family takes time and must be completed in advance of the pregnancy. So forward planning is required if this is to be possible. Testing would normally be carried out with the, at least tacit, expectation that high risk fetuses would be aborted. This raises moral questions about terminating pregnancies, and will only be considered by certain couples. But will those couples be making free choices, or will they be under pressure to terminate the pregnancy even if the result is not entirely clear?

In the past some geneticist's advice for couples at risk not to reproduce smacked of 'social engineering' and conjures up memories of the eugenics movements of the 1890s and Nazi Germany. So there will have to be a balance struck between the case for selective termination of high risk fetuses on the one hand and parental autonomy on the other. But if a couple request prenatal testing and then decide not to proceed with termination, who has a right to that information about the genetic status of the resulting child? What affect will this knowledge have on the parents' relationship with their child? When and by whom should the child be informed of the test result? What right does a future spouse have to that information? Therapeutic abortions on genetic grounds are usually for inherited conditions that produce profound abnormalities by the time of birth or early in life. In the case of Huntington's disease, even a high risk individual might not be expected to develop symptoms for three decades or more. In what way does this alter decision-making?

The problem of suicide and Huntington's disease is an acute one. Surveys of people at risk of Huntington's disease show a high family history of psychiatric hospital admissions (thirty five per cent) and suicide or parasuicide (thirty-seven per cent).[9] Recently Farrer[13] reported that about six per cent of HD patients known to one national case register had committed suicide and twenty-eight per cent had made one or more suicidal attempt. Over two-thirds of at-risk persons expected that they would become depressed if predictive tests results were 'positive', and between five and twenty-one per cent said they would commit suicide.[14,15]

What should the professional response be in the case of the person who discovers that he or she has inherited the gene and then threatens to commit suicide? Should the person be prevented from carrying out this threat, if necessary using compulsory admission to hospital? Or should 'benign neglect' (or other suicide-encouraging strategies) be offered?[14] Is suicide in these circumstances a dignified and rational solution to an increasingly deteriorating life or the act of a demented person? Kessler concludes a moving letter[14] by giving his personal rule of thumb – to treat suicidal gestures as cries for help to find reasons to live. He tries to promote conditions in which the life of the impaired person is protected and the coping skills of caretakers improved. Farrer,[15] replying to Kessler, states that is it 'unconscionable to fail to anticipate the possibility of suicidal behaviour in the at-risk individual who hears an unfavourable test result'. She has argued that any presymptomatic testing programme must include adequate provisions for pre- and post-test counselling as well as long-term psychological support.

Controlling genetic testing

Having considered some of the medical, ethical, moral, legal and psychological issues involved in just one disease (HD) and attempts to improve the lot of those at risk through the offer of presymptomatic and antenatal testing, it is necessary to look forward and, in particular, to consider what part present and future legislation might play in helping and protecting all those involved.

Presymptomatic testing should only be carried out on adults who are able to give informed consent. This statement may sound clear enough, but the whole question of what constitutes informed consent has recently been debated. Thus those under the age at which proper consent can be given must be excluded. In some American states pre-natal testing is banned because the fetus (being tested) is unable to give informed consent.

The subjects must have the test result protected by law, and this must not be available to employers. There are many medical conditions (from pre-senile dementia to hypothyroidism) and behaviour patterns (drug and alcohol abuse) that might impair a person's ability to function safely at work. All of these (including HD) should be picked up at an early stage by vigilant employers on work and attendance record. There is no need for mandatory reporting of a positive result indicating the probable inheritance of a condition which might not manifest itself for decades.

Other family members involved indirectly in the test procedure by donating blood for testing also need to be sure of legal safeguards. The confidentiality of their samples, which may be stored deep frozen indefinitely, must be protected by law. Such storage arrangements should be controlled and inspected. Their records should be stored apart from the normal records to avoid the possibility of chance accidental disclosures to another person, or to themselves. While it would seem undesirable to compel family members to give blood samples, there is the question of the protection of those who may be vulnerable to pressure. In particular the elderly, the very young, especially those being considered for adoption, and those whose intellect is impaired by HD. This is probably adequately covered by the need to obtain informed consent before taking blood samples. But in the case of those already affected and perhaps nearing the end of their life, who are incapable of giving informed consent, consent of their doctor should be obtained.

Prenatal testing without therapeutic termination poses a particular problem for the protection of the child from premature disclosure of the test result. Nevertheless that child does have a right to that test information at an appropriate age. Full pre-disclosure counselling should be provided. Thus the 'positive' result of prenatal testing should carry legal safeguards, perhaps in the form of a contract between the testing clinic and the parents. Existing abortion legislation permits termination where there is a substantial risk that if the child were born it would suffer from such physical or mental abnormalities as to be seriously handicapped. But what about the case of HD? These conditions usually apply to diseases that will be present at birth or in childhood, not illnesses that will only appear after decades of productive life. And yet it seems eminently desirable for that individual family and for society that, if there is a possibility of producing only 'normal' offspring who can lead normal lives free from the worries of developing an incurable illness which may be passed on to future generations, then it should be possible within the law for that course to be followed.

Ideally close relatives, especially spouses, should be present at pre-test counselling sessions. But what if they are excluded? Do they have a right to know the test result? While there may appear to be a prima facie case for mandatory disclosure, this cannot easily be justified through legislation. The spouse who refuses to disclose the test result may well be putting his marriage in jeopardy. Decisions about further pregnancies may well be influenced by the assumption that failure to disclose is indicative of a positive result. But what about the right of children to know the results of their parent's test? Providing the parent is prepared to give blood, tests can be performed without disclosure of the parent's result to the child. In the case of the child's test being positive, then the parent's status can be inferred.

Finally, the legislation surrounding suicide and mental illness appears clear. If an individual intends to kill himself, but is not showing any sign of a mental disorder defined by the various Mental Health Acts, then there is no recourse to mental health legislation to 'protect' him. If he is suffering from mental deterioration because of HD to such a degree that he is mentally impaired in the meaning of the Acts, then he can be compulsorily admitted to and detained in hospital for his own protection and treatment. Treatment in this case would be nursing care rather than specific medical intervention. In Scotland more than fifty at-risk individuals have been tested[16] and with the approach of the end of one year follow-up, there have been no suicides. Most of those who have undergone the test are sure that they have made the correct decision, even those for whom the test proved 'positive'. The removal of the uncertainty is what they value most, and the possibility of planning more sensibly for the future.

Some of these dilemmas will be removed by the development of a test for the HD gene. This will remove the need for any other members of the family to be involved. But the questions of confidentiality, counselling and termination will remain.

Notes

1. Emery, 'The Principles of Genetic Counselling' in *Psychological aspects of genetic counselling* (Emery and Pullen eds) London and New York: Academic Press, 1984.
2. Emery, *An introduction to Recombinant DNA* pp. 122–127. Chichester: John Wiley, 1985.

3. Kessler, 'The psychological foundations of genetic counseling' in *Genetic Counseling: Psychological Dimensions* pp. 17–33. New York: Academic Press, 1979.
4. Went, 'Ethical issues policy statement on Huntington's disease molecular genetics predictive test' (27) *Journal of Medical Genetics* (1990) pp. 34–38.
5. Emery et al 'Prospective study of genetic counselling' *British Medical Journal* (1979) (1) 1253–1256.
6. Falek, 'Sequential aspects of coping and other issues in decision making in genetic counselling' in *Psychological aspects of genetic counselling* (Emery and Pullen eds) London and New York: Academic Press, 1984.
7. Wexler, 'Huntington's disease and other late onset genetic disorders' in *Psychological aspects of genetic counselling* (Emery and Pullen eds) London and New York: Academic Press, 1984.
8. Yoxen, *Unnatural selection* p. 142. London, Heinemann, 1986.
9. Kessler, 'Psychiatric implications of presymptomatic testing for Huntington's disease' (57) *American Journal of Orthopsychiatry* (1987) pp. 212–219.
10. Guesella et al 'A polymorphic DNA marker genetically linked to Huntington's disease' (306) *Nature* (1983) pp. 950–52.
11. Smurl and Weaver 'Presymptomatic testing for Huntington's chorea: guidelines for moral and social accountability' (26) *American Journal of Medical Genetics* (1987) pp. 247–257.
12. Lamport, 'Presymptomatic testing for Huntington's chorea: Ethical and legal issues' (26) *American Journal of Medical Genetics* (1987) pp. 307–314.
13. Farrer 'Suicide and attempted suicide in Huntington's disease: implications for preclinical persons at risk' (24) *American Journal of Medical Genetics* (1986) pp. 305–311.
14. Kessler, 'Letter to the editor: the dilemma of suicide and Huntington's disease' (26) *American Journal of Medical Genetics* (1987) pp. 315–317.
15. Farrer, 'Letter to the editor: response to Kessler: suicide and presymptomatic testing in Huntington's disease' (26) *American Journal of Medical Genetics* (1987) pp. 319–320.
16. Brock et al 'Predictive testing for Huntington's disease with linked DNA markers' *Lancet* (1989) pp. 463–466.

4. The family and life and death decisions
David Meyers

The family has always played an important role in life and death medical treatment decisions. As society's most important institution this is hardly surprising. The family is expected to decide these matters in a socially and legally acceptable way. The family is presumed to have love and affection for, and knowledge of, the person in need of medical care.

Generally, the law both in the United Kingdom and in the United States presumes that life and death treatment decisions are best left to the judgement of the family and the physicians where the patient is unable to speak clearly and informatively for himself because of some incapacity. That incapacity may be the result of age, injury, illness or treatment. Even where the patient is capable of deciding, the family is often consulted and its views, though not conclusive, may be influential in the decision-making process.

Life and death treatment decisions may confront the family at different times in the natural evolution of its members from conception to birth, during life, and finally, as death nears. Members of the family may not all enjoy equal rights. For example, the decision whether to lawfully abort a fetus is one the mother is entitled to make, regardless of the views of the father.[1] A child, even though still a minor, may consent to an abortion without the consent of either parent where she is mature enough to make an informed decision herself.[2] The same is true for any other lawful medical treatment.[3]

Historically, in Scotland, the doctrine of *patria potestas* gave the father alone the power to make medical treatment decisions for his young children before they reached the age of minority, twelve for girls, fourteen for boys.[4] Modern courts recognize the authority of either parent to make such decisions. Nonetheless, reasonable efforts are customarily made to ascertain the views of both parents unless an emergency situation makes this impractical.[5]

Where treatment is required for an incapacitated adult, the spouse will normally be looked to by the attending physicians for consent to treat.[6] If other family members are available their views will be considered by the conscientious practitioner. Normally, the views of the family members will align. However, this is not always true and in such cases efforts should be made to resolve any differences before significant decisions on treatment are made.[7] If informal or institutional efforts fail, then resort to the courts for guidance at such times is appropriate.

Sometimes family is unavailable or uninterested in the patient. If extended family is available – niece or nephew or cousin, for example – they normally will be preferred guardians to strangers. They may be the closest available relative and as such enjoy a presumed right to consent to medical treatment for the incapable patient.[8] The California Supreme Court, in a 1972 decision defending the disclosure of all material information standard for patient informed consent, concluded,[9]

> If the patient is a minor or incompetent, the authority to consent is transferred to the patient's legal guardian or closest available relative.

The Court could be accused of oversimplifying the process in such cases. However, the dearth of legal precedent dealing with family or other surrogate medical decision-making at that time offers ample explanation for the statement. In 1972 no 'right to die' cases had reached the appellate courts for explication of who decides for the incompetent patient and by what standards. Over these past nearly twenty years the law and medical practice have been undergoing significant development. Recently, there has developed a greater recognition that those most likely to know what the patient would want done may not always be the immediate family. The criterion here should be who can most accurately and sincerely tell the physicians what the patient would want done, or not done, given the circumstances at hand. In one recent case this was found to be the religious superior of a Catholic Brother of the Society of Mary.[10] In other cases it may be a long-time friend or companion. The law should allow flexibility for such non-familial surrogates where they are best able to represent the patient's viewpoint. This can be done while still retaining the normal presumption in favour of the spouse, parents or other available family.

To best understand the development of the law in this area, some discussion of the relationship, in practice, between treating physicians and family should be explored. From there we will look at specific family treatment issues dealing with the competent patient fully able to decide, as well as standards of decision-making for those incapable of deciding, including adults, children and newborn.

The traditional paternalistic approach of physicians to the patient and family

Until recent times, physicians as a rule approached life and death decisions from a largely paternalistic perspective.[11] Limited means of sustaining life in the face of terminal and incurable illness made this approach easy to carry out and raised few objections among patients or their families. However, as technological advances in medical care and treatments for the seriously ill occurred, the options available to the decision-makers became much greater. Cardio-pulmonary resuscitation, the artificial respirator and new drugs allowed continuation of circulation and respiration in those previously doomed to die upon cessation of spontaneous respiration or circulation. Modern surgical techniques offer new hope for previously hopeless conditions.

Typically, before these advances there was no real choice available to the family. The doctor did what he or she could to preserve the life of the patient. An adrenaline injection or some other stimulant might be given to a victim of cardiac arrest. Little else was available. Where cancer was present, surgery was a possibility in certain cases. If the physician recommended it, normally the family went along. Death could not be interminably delayed, nor was the cost of medical care anything like the frightening magnitude of today's charges for extended hospitalization, complicated surgeries, or other 'hi-tech' techniques such as radiation therapy, chemotherapy, chronic dialysis, open heart surgery, or bone marrow and other sophisticated organ transplantation.

Several other reasons explain why paternalism traditionally played a much stronger role in medical treatment decisions than it does today. First, as mentioned, far fewer choices in care existed and thus there was considerably less need for non-physician decision-makers. Second, medicine had a certain aura about it. Physicians neither by training nor by practice encouraged family or, for that matter, patient involvement in the decision-making process. They knew the treatment options available, what was indicated for the patient and they pursued what 'had to be done' or what they deemed to be the 'best thing' for their patient. The physician, with few exceptions, was a self-confident, authoritarian individual who felt he knew what needed to be done and did it.

Patients, even in today's legal and social atmosphere of patient autonomy and self-determination, are still as a rule quite happy to have their physician do what he or she thinks is best. After all, the linchpin of the physician-patient relationship has always been trust: trust that the physician can be relied upon to exercise good, educated judgment and to do what is best for the patient.

Following World War II, the proliferation of technological advances in medicine brought to the fore the need and the responsibility to decide what treatment to employ, when, and for how long. Choices between alternative treatments became more complicated and subtle: whether to remove the total breast in the event of a cancerous tumour, or only the tumour itself; whether to treat cardiovascular disease invasively – by angioplasty and, if necessary, bypass open heart surgery – or conservatively with blood thinners, dietary and other lifestyle changes; whether to put a terminally and incurably ill patient through surgery, chemotherapy or other difficult and painful treatment; whether to commence or to continue use of an artificial respirator in 'hopeless' cases. The list goes on and seems to grow daily.

A greater social and legal awareness of individual self-determination – reflected in the United States by the civil rights legislation of the 1960s and worldwide by enactment of codes such as the 1965 Declaration of Helsinki to protect human rights and against the abuses of medical experimentation – elevated the importance of the patient's right to decide on his or her own treatment. This has manifested itself in judicial recognition of the so-called 'informed consent' doctrine.[12] The doctrine was really nothing more than an attempt by American judges and legal scholars to ensure meaningful exercise of the indivdual's right to self-determination in medical care.

The role of the media and a populace perhaps overly preoccupied with sickness, health and its own mortality has encouraged much greater lay participation in medical treatment decisions. Much of the 'mystery' of medicine has been exposed to the public eye. The result is that many seem to consider medicine a science, not an art, rather than a melding of both. In this view medicine is seen as a means of extending life nearly indefinitely by simply selecting the right drug, procedure or device to employ.

Finally, the threat of legal liability for untoward result has become much more real in recent years, particularly in the United States, as a result of the above phenomena, the increased technical challenges in the practice of medicine brought about by the plethora of new drugs and procedures, and by a sometimes unrealistic expectation by the patient of the abilities of modern medicine to cure or prolong life. This threat has in turn encouraged physicians to seek to insulate themselves from liability in several ways, including that of informing patients more fully, to gain their consent and involvement in the treatment decision. When the patient understands and consents to treatment, he or she is, presumably, less likely to sue over that treatment, and if so, less likely to prevail.

All of these influences have eroded the paternalistic, 'benign authoritarian' practice of medicine. The result has been a greater role for the patient, or his family, in deciding upon treatment. This, as might be expected, is particularly true with life and death decisions. We look now at those roles.

The role of the family

It should not be inferred from anything said that the family has not normally been consulted concerning treatment decisions for those loved ones unable to decide for themselves. In such situations, the physician has normally advised the available immediate family what he or she proposed to do. The family would normally concur. The options were limited and the path to be taken usually quite clear.

While not clearly articulated in the law, the practice of the physician and family deciding upon treatment for the patient lacking capacity to decide for himself has been respected and not legally challenged. It has been accepted *sub silentio* by the law, there being little need to articulate in judicial precedent what was commonly done without reported or suspected abuse, appeared to work well in practice, and met with society's approval. After all, who was normally available and in a better position to know what the patient would want done, or what was 'best' for him, than his immediate family? While certain estrangements were not necessarily uncommon among certain family members, the family normally represented loved ones, who were available, were providing care and affection for the ill patient, and were interested in his or her cure.

In recent times, there has been a more clear need to recognize who can be looked to to decide on treatment for an incompetent patient – one without the capacity to decide for himself. A number of courts have recognized that, absent the judicial appointment of a guardian or conservator, the available family or next of kin is the proper substitute decision-maker for the patient.[7] Courts have also opined that no guardian need normally be appointed, even where the treatment proposed to be withheld or withdrawn is life-sustaining; the family should be able to decide.[13]

This is not to say, however, that the family should enjoy unquestioned authority to decide for the incompetent patient-family member. The presumption of love and affection and the belief they will act in the patient's best interests may not be borne out in certain cases. Potential inheritance may slant the charitable viewpoint of spouse or child, particularly where the patient is incurably ill. There may be an unwillingness to shoulder the financial or emotional burden of caring for the patient, making a decision to allow death to occur more likely. There may be a natural tendency to decide based on what the family wants done, which may not always coincide with what the patient would want done. For these reasons, or others, the physicians, some family members or a social worker may on occasion feel the appointment of a guardian, perhaps one unrelated to the patient, is preferable. In rare instances, the court may be petitioned to settle, or choose between, disputes among family members concerning care.[14] The courts must remain accessible to resolve such cases of familial dispute or disagreement, suspected motive, bad faith, or bad practice.

The presumption that the family can decide life and death decisions for an incompetent member is a proper and practical one. The vast majority of those nearing death are looked after by their family. Absent the concerns mentioned above, there is no need and no appropriateness for the legal machinery to become involved. The family is normally available, concerned and caring. Just as we as a society look to the family to support and nurture the birth and rearing of the young, so too do we look to it to care for and ease the dying of its members whether young or old. This is a fundamental obligation of the family. It is best equipped to fulfill it. It, presumptively, knows the patient best, his wishes and his needs. No other institution in society is as suitable, unless the family is unavailable, in disagreement or uncaring.

While involving a disinterested, court-appointed guardian or conservator may lend needed objectivity and fairness in selected, atypical situations, it may also be an expensive, time consuming and embarrassing intrusion by a public, institutional process into an intensely intimate and personal setting.[15] For this reason, the goal of the law and medical practice should be to encourage substitute decision-making by the concerned available family or other appropriate surrogate wherever possible. This has been and should continue to be the norm. There could, however, be clearer legal recognition given to the powers and responsibilities of the family in these matters in order to make both caregivers and family members more comfortable. Surprisingly little legal precedent supporting the role of the family in such matters existed until recently.

It would be desirable if legislation made it clear that in the absence of the express appointment of a proxy or agent by the patient while capable of doing so, or unless and until the appointment of a legal guardian, the family is presumed to have the right to consent or refuse consent to treatment for a member unable to do so himself. Some jurisdictions may wish to specify an order of priority for decision-making within the family: spouse, adult children, parents, brothers and sisters seems logical as a starting point. Some may wish to provide mechanisms for dispute resolution. Other surrogates may at times be preferable to family based on their knowledge of and caring for the patient.[10]

The adult patient able to decide for himself

If the patient is able to decide for himself, as a rule the family cannot legally challenge or contradict that decision, no matter how unpopular or unwise in their eyes.[16] The family may try to persuade the patient to change his or her mind, but they have no right to overrule.

Bodily integrity and self-determination are both individual rights and freedoms. They belong to the holder, not to his family, if he is able to exercise those rights. A spouse, or other family member may not overrule or second guess the patient's informed decision to refuse treatment even though death will ensue.[17] Rare exceptions may exist where the patient can be cured and will leave uncared-for dependents if treatment is not given, or where the patient asks another to actively aid or abet a suicide because no terminal and incurable condition is present.

The standards of proxy decision-making to be employed by the family or other surrogate

Family members are normally felt to be the best proxy decision-makers for an incompetent patient because of two basic presumptions: that they know best what the patient would decide given the circumstances at hand; and, secondly, that they want that which is in the best interests of the patient. These presumptions – in that order of priority – form the basis for the standards by which proxy decision-makers – whether family or otherwise – should act in electing for or against particular care or treatment for the patient.[18]

In a democratic society, few would argue that the greatest possible respect should be given to individual freedom of choice. Maximizing freedom of choice means recognizing individual self-determination to the greatest extent feasible, consistent with the good of society and the avoidance of harm to others.[19] This in turn means letting the patient capable of exercising free choice decide on his or her own medical treatment, so long as it does not cause harm to others. The task then, when the patient does not possess capacity to decide, is to replicate to the greatest extent reasonably possible the choice the patient would make if capable of doing so. This maximizes individual self-determination for all patients, carries out the reasonable expectations of the patient and gives assurance to all that their wishes will be honoured, if they are known. The challenge here is to know what the patient would have wanted.

A relevant written directive from the patient while competent to decide is obviously best evidence to his or her desires, but may often be lacking. Candid discussions among family members or patient and prospective proxy are desirable and helpful, but a natural reluctance to talk of death or one's mortality may discourage these discussions.[20] What the patient says about public figures or others being sustained in various degrees of vegetative or medical-technological dependent existence may shed valuable light on the wishes of the patient if such a condition were to befall him.[10]

Often there may only be a 'sense' of what the patient would want done based on knowledge by the family of his or her religious views, philosophy of life, internal constitution and self-image and other, rather subjective attitudes or generalized comments.[21] Here it will be much more difficult to know how the patient would have decided under perhaps ambiguous or clearly unanticipated health circumstances and much more likely that the personal views of the proxy will largely colour the decision.

Pragmatism and experience tells us that often it will not be clear what the patient, if able, would have decided. The particular incapacitating malady or trauma, far less the proposed treatment, may never have been discussed or contemplated. For this reason a second standard, a backup standard, of proxy decision-making must be available to protect the patient and aid the family. This is also necessary for those never able to express their views: the very young or the congenitally incapacitated.

What has evolved as this backup standard is best interests.[18] Lacking awareness or conviction as to what decision the patient would have actually made, the next choice most agree must be that which is best for him, in his best interests. While imperfect, this allows a decision to be made rather than inaction to decide the issue. It also gives notice to others how their care will be decided absent knowledge of what they would decide. It lends reassurance and fairness to the proxy decision-making process. Although doing what others – physicians and family, or other proxy – perceive to be in the patient's best interests may well not be what he or she would actually decide if able to do so, it is a *reasonable* criterion of decision-making and one, if defined clearly, that presumably *most* would make if able to do so.

Doing what is in the presumed best interests of the patient is doing what is reasonable under the circumstances. Doing what is reasonable is doing what most reasonable people would do under the circumstances. Thus, the odds are this is what the patient would want done. In a society that imposes throughout our life both civil and, at times, criminal responsibility upon us for failing to act like the proverbial and mythical 'reasonable man', it is understandable and not inconsistent to have our medical fate decided based on a similar standard.[22]

The President's Commission Report[18] gave doctors a workable formula for applying the best interests standard. By its formulation, a treatment is in the best interests of the patient if it is *proportionate* treatment: that is, if the reasonably anticipated benefits it promises in the view of the patient outweigh the burdens attendant to it. If the burdens outweigh the benefits, it is *disproportionate* treatment and not in the patient's best interests. The problem remains, however, of knowing the views of the incapacitated patient since it is still the patient's evaluation of benefits and burdens that should control. Without such knowledge, resort must be had to the perspective of the so-called 'reasonable patient', an equally mythical figure to the reasonable man of tort law.

A landmark California case, which threw out criminal charges against two physicians who had authorized removal of artificial respiration, nutrition and hydration from a comatose patient, provided general treatment 'benefits' criteria.[6] They include:

1. the relief of suffering;

2. the preservation or restoration of functioning;
3. the quality of the possible extension of life; and,
4. the extent of the possible extension of life.

While these are helpful parameters, the best interests test remains elusive and not easily defined. Most courts have accepted it for lack of a better standard. Like Supreme Court Justice Stewart's oft-quoted definitional reference to obscenity as, 'I know it when I see it!', this 'best interests' standard has obviously been relied on by families and doctors for years without any apparent abuse despite its lack of definitional precision. With eight of ten Americans and six of ten Britons dying in hospital, with life-sustaining technologies readily available, decisions must of necessity be made on a daily basis in many instances where the views of the patient are either unknown or not relevant.

Two state supreme courts have recently rejected reliance on the 'best interests' standard as illusory and an inappropriate basis upon which to withdraw life sustaining treatment, regardless of the hopelessness of that treatment.[23] The problem with this criticism is that it, in effect, forces the decision of continued treatment in all cases where the wishes of the patient are not known. This may well do more violence to the dignity and actual preferences of the patient, if known, than the best interests standard. It may also result in unwise use of limited medical resources and prolongation of suffering or humiliation for patient and family in many cases.

Another recent court decision concluded that the 'best interests' standard does not fulfill a patient's right of privacy, because it does not reflect what the patient himself would actually choose to do in the exercise of that right. The court characterized it as,

> a test under which the surrogate decision-maker seems to make the decision which a public referendum or a benign leader would reach. We cannot afford to confuse the patient's right of privacy with a public opinion poll.[24]

This viewpoint assumes the patient who has not expressed himself would always want to receive life-sustaining treatment, regardless of its relative benefits and burdens. The effect is to always require the continuation of such treatment. This, it is submitted, far more often than not will frustrate the privacy rights of the individual rather than respecting them. When treatment is highly invasive or unpleasant and fundamentally detracts from the patient's personal dignity, only to briefly prolong a terminal and incurable condition, few indeed would want it. Absent some disagreement, ill motive, bad faith or uncertainty, these decisions are properly, practically and ethically made by the patient's loved ones and his attending physicians. It is inappropriate for courts to interfere with their own prohibitory views in the absence of reported abuse or legislative standards. The criminal law provides adequate protective backdrop to such decisions to guard against ill motive, bad faith or intentional wrongdoing. In addition, the 'best interests' standard has long controlled decisions by parents on all forms of treatment for their children. It does not seem inappropriate for spouses, grown children or other surrogates to apply it to adult loved ones no longer able to decide for themselves.

These issues point out the need to express oneself or to appoint a proxy to decide for oneself before one is incapable of doing so. The Durable Power of Attorney for Health Care legislation[25] now adopted in much of the US seeks to do this by allowing one to designate another to decide *all* health care questions if and when one is no longer able to do so himself. This includes the right to refuse life-sustaining treatment.

The US Supreme Court was recently called upon to decide if life-sustaining medical treatment may be withdrawn by family and physicians who have decided it is not in the best interests of the patient incompetent to decide for himself. The Court held that states, if they wish, may require clear and convincing evidence – a stringent legal standard – that a terminally or incurably ill patient would not want life-sustaining treatment continued before authorizing its removal.[21] Thus, in such cases, states may legitimately prohibit the best interests standard for proxy decision-making.

The adult patient unable to decide for himself

If the patient is unable to understand the general nature and purpose of the treatment, its consequences (risks and benefits), and the feasible alternatives to it, he cannot give an informed consent to it.[26] If the patient cannot give an informed consent, then he is unable to decide for himself. This does not mean that to consent the patient must be independent, not have a guardian or conservator appointed to manage his affairs, not be institutionalized in a mental facility, or be certified as legally competent to contract or care for himself.[27] It means only that the patient must understand what the treatment is all about at least in general terms, including its risks and benefits, before he or she may consent to it. Consent to treatment to be valid and meaningful to both patient and physician must be free and must be informed, or it is illusory.

Courts in the United States have given families or other surrogates the right to make life and death decisions, in consultation with the attending physicians, in many instances.[6,7,9,13] Those instances include: withdrawing artificially supplied food, water and respiration for those in a persistent vegetative state (permanent coma),[6,13] or those suffering in the advanced stages of a terminal and incurable illness involving severe and permanent mental and physical deterioration;[7] withdrawing hemodialysis from a hopelessly comatose patient, whether young or old;[28] and electing against highly invasive surgery, or other treatment, such as chemotherapy,[29] limb amputation,[30] or in the face of severe congenital anomalies, which will cause a newborn infant pain and not correct an inability to 'interact with her environment or with other people'.[31]

The family has an important role in proxy decision-making because discussions about life and death, if they have occurred, will likely have occurred with a family member. Of course, there will be instances where a dear friend will be closer to the patient and more knowledgeable of his or her wishes than any family member. This, for example, may be true with some homosexuals suffering from AIDS who, unfortunately, because of the disease or their sexual orientation are not infrequently estranged from their families and unmarried.

As a rule, physicians will feel comfortable relying on the family or other surrogate decision-maker who has a close relationship to the incompetent patient. If, however, there is suspected ill motive or neglect, uncertainty as to the best interests of the patient or what he would want done under the circumstances, a referral to the local social welfare agency may be appropriate, or the court appointment of a legal guardian or conservator with specific, court-authorized powers to decide on treatment.

The newborn

The family may be called upon to make life and death decisions concerning a just born child. Normally this will be automatic and not a cause of disagreement. However, where the newborn suffers severe birth defects, the parents may not wish to authorize medical treatment necessary for survival. Physicians have acknowledged for many years that they do not 'strive officiously' to keep such infants alive. This practice has been accepted by most physicians and parents, although its legality has been not without considerable uncertainty.[32]

In 1982, the Indiana courts permitted parents to elect against surgical correction of an oesophageal obstruction in a Down's syndrome baby. Although not publicly disclosed, the child apparently also suffered from other, serious, probably life-threatening congenital anomalies, including one of the heart. Considerable outcry followed publicity about the case, particularly among the so-called 'pro-life' political groups. The Reagan administration responded by promulgating regulations for treatment of handicapped newborns.[33] Those regulations, as eventually revised and adopted in 1985,[34] bar the withholding of 'medically indicated' treatment from handicapped newborns. The idea here is to leave room for the exercise of reasonable medical judgement. Exceptions are provided where the infant is irreversibly comatose, treatment would only prolong inevitable death, or where treatment would be virtually futile in enabling the child to survive and would under the circumstances be 'inhumane.'

Despite some conflicting legal precedents, few seem to argue with the notion that aggressive or invasive medical treatment may properly and humanely be withheld or withdrawn in certain very limited circumstances of severe handicap. Professor Mason and I have suggested that the parents should be able to say no to treatment, other than basic and humane nursing care, where it has been confirmed that,

a. death is highly probable, regardless of treatment, within the first year of the infant's life; or
b. there is no reasonable possibility the infant will be able to participate to any degree in human relationships requiring some interaction or responses; or,
c. treatment cannot alleviate an intolerable level of chronic pain or discomfort, making continued treatment inhumane.[35]

There can be general guidelines only. There are all degrees and variations of congenital abnormalities. Some, such as Down's syndrome, can be very mild and not adversely impact the child's opportunity for love and enjoyment of life. Others, such as severe cases of spina bifida, offer little hope the child will be free from pain or able to relate in any meaningful way to his or her environment or those around him or her. Parents also have different levels of tolerance and capacity to love and nurture such children. Parents also are responsible not only for the birth of their child, but also for the financial and emotional burdens of nurturing and raising that child to take his or her place in society. Accordingly, these cases are properly best left to be decided with compassion by the attending physicians and the parents after thoughtful and competent assessment of the infant's degree of handicap and prognosis. The law must allow the participants a reasonable amount of flexibility of judgement and understanding in such highly personalized and private decisions.[36] Families and physicians have made these decisions compassionately in the past, with very few cases of reported abuse, and there is no reason why they should not be permitted to do so in the future. The criminal law as written remains a threat, as it should to deter abuse. As administered, by judges and juries, it does not appear to have unduly restricted parental discretion or clinical judgement in these cases, nor to have reached unfair results in those rare instances when it has been imposed.[37]

Children

Children present a special case. If they are able to decide on treatment for themselves, they may do so. No particular age needs to be attained. The question is one of understanding, not chronological age. Just as with adults, if the child is able to understand the general nature and purpose of the treatment, its reasonably expected risks and benefits, as well as the feasible alternatives to it, then he or she may consent, or refuse consent, to it.[26] These are the necessary elements to giving an informed consent. Duff has opined that most children by the age of fourteen are able to make medical treatment decisions, including life and death decisions.[38] Many states require the consent of children fourteen years of age or older before a guardian can impose treatment, except that immediately needed to avoid death or serious disability. Some states grant children the statutory right to consent to certain kinds of treatment thought essential to the public good – as for communicable disease, alcohol or drug addiction, or sexual abuse – at a particular age, such as twelve.[39] However, these special statutes probably do not dispense with the need to obtain an 'informed' consent from the patient or his guardian, absent an emergency obviating that requirement.

At a rather tender age a child will be able to give an informed consent to simple and low risk procedures – infectious disease immunization, cleansing and closing a surface wound, removing tooth decay. As treatment becomes more complicated or risky, or the risks and benefits more closely balanced, the added maturity and understanding that normally comes with age is necessary for an informed consent.

Adulthood is generally recognized in American law at age eighteen (ability to marry, to vote, to contract, to be conscripted). However, few 'children' need await that age to be entitled to give or refuse informed consent to treatment of any kind, including that with consequences of life or death.

The picture is clouded somewhat by the great deference given to parental decision-making in American law. For generations the courts have recognized that the parental right to raise and nurture children is one of Constitutional dimension and one jealously protected.[40] It seems to be rooted in two concepts: one, that parents, as a matter of personal right and privacy, should be left alone to raise their own children the way they choose to the greatest extent reasonable possible; and, two, that parents carry out important social responsibilities in raising children that should not, as a matter of policy, be lightly tampered with by others. Despite this, once the child demonstrates the ability to decide for himself, he may decide without parental interference.

Where the parental right to decide remains because the child does not have sufficient understanding to decide the treatment question presented, parents must act in the best interests of their children. While they enjoy substantial discretion in deciding what is best for their children, they cannot neglect or abuse their child's physical well-being.[41]

Many cases have presented the issue of whether parents because of their religious convictions may refuse blood or surgery for their child, who needs it to avoid likely death or serious disability. The answer is no. The state will not hesitate, in the exercise of its inherent jurisdiction as *parens patriae*, to assume custody of such a child in order to authorize the medical treatment proposed.[42] This is not to say that because doctors think treatment should be given to a child that parents cannot say no. If the likely benefits of treatment are debated or unclear, or the burdens or risks posed by it are substantial, social welfare authorities are much less likely to be informed or to intervene. The same is even more true for the courts.

If the treatment proposed for the child is characterized as life-sustaining in nature or purpose, the pressure will be much greater to legally intervene in the face of parental refusal. However, where parents choose one form of reasonable treatment over that of another, but different reasonable treatment, courts are unlikely to overrule that choice. Courts have held, for example, that parents may elect conservative, non-invasive metabolic therapy for their child suffering from Hodgkin's Disease, rather than recommended radiation and chemotherapy,[43] may elect against surgery carrying a five per cent to ten per cent risk of mortality to correct a congenital heart defect likely to worsen if untreated and cause death within about twenty years,[44] and may elect to conservatively treat a severely deformed newborn with nutrition, antibiotics and other nursing care rather than authorizing a brain shunt and spinal defect closure.[45]

The law does not demand perfection, because we cannot meet such a standard. The parents' duty to their child is one of *reasonable* care. Accordingly, where they act reasonably, by 'responsibly' deciding between two accepted schools of medical thought, they incur no liability and give the state no cause to intervene against their wishes.[46] One court has identified the factors that must be evaluated before the wishes of the parents concerning the treatment of their child are overruled:

> The State should examine the seriousness of the harm the child is suffering or the substantial likelihood that he will suffer serious harm; the evaluation for the treatment by the medical profession; the risks involved in medically treating the child; and the expressed preferences of the child. Of course, the underlying consideration is the child's welfare and whether his best interests will be served by the medical treatment.[44]

Where the decision of parents to refuse treatment for their child, or to pursue a particular treatment, is disputed by doctors or public authorities, certain values and rights clearly collide. Those are parental autonomy and privacy on the one hand, professional treatment standards and the best interests of the child on the other. Thus, looking solely to the child's best interest is not the end of the analysis. A comparison and balancing of interests must take place in such cases. The legal precedents are more understandable when viewed in this light.

While courts take little pause in ordering clearly accepted treatment felt necessary by competent medical practitioners to avoid death or serious and permanent physical impairment to a child,[47] they are loath to overrule parents in most other, less clear situations. For example, courts have refused to overrule parents and to order a spinal fusion to allow a seventeen-year-old polio victim to walk,[48] amputation to remove the burdensome and grossly deformed arm of an eleven-year old,[49] surgery to correct a fourteen-year old's cleft palate and hairlip,[50] psychiatric help for a disturbed child,[51] sterilization unless other means of contraception are inadequate to preserve the physical or mental health of the minor,[52] or continuation of a respirator for a child in persistent vegetative state without hope of return to consciousness.[53]

Absent those instances where treatment is felt necessary to save the life of the infant, very few cases have reached the US courts for resolution. Some courts have essentially said they will only overrule the treatment wishes of the parents where the treatment refused is necessary to prevent the child's death.[48] While extreme, such pronouncements highlight the strong reluctance of courts to second guess parents, except in the clearest of cases. Aside from such generally 'hands off' statements by the judiciary, other reasons help to explain the dearth of such cases. First and foremost, most parents do what is best for their children, follow the treatment recommendations of their physician and give no cause for involvement of the courts. Second, it is fair to say that physicians generally recognize the wishes of the parents and the discretion they enjoy and are unlikely to contact social welfare or child protective authorities except in cases of clear neglect.[36] Third, most states have reporting requirements for cases of suspected child abuse or abandonment and the attention of the authorities is an effective means of persuading proper care. Custody can be removed from the parents where necessary to protect the child. Finally, the threat of the criminal law remains a strong deterrent to child abuse or neglect. Homicide liability can be imposed if death ensues.[41]

Conclusions

The family has a role to play in all life and death decisions concerning its members. This role is a natural and healthy one that has long been recognized for the family. Where the person to be treated is capable of giving an informed consent to treatment, based on an understanding of its general nature and purpose, the reasonably likely risks and benefits posed by it, and the alternatives to it, he or she may decide for himself or herself whether to pursue or forego the treatment. That is his or her right, regardless of age, infirmity, prognosis or legal status. Here the family can seek to convince of an alternative course, or confirm the wisdom of the patient's choice, as it wishes. The family should be helpful and supportive, but should recognize it has no legal or moral entitlement to overrule the patient's free and informed choice.

Often the family member will be incapable of deciding for himself. This will be true of the newborn. It will also be true of some children, normally when certain complex or risky treatment is proposed or they are of tender years without great understanding. Some adults will be unable to decide. The reasons will be varied: congenital abnormality, illness, injury, age or medication.

Where the patient is unable to decide, the family must strive to honour him by authorizing what he would want done (or not done) under the circumstances. Incompetency should not rob the patient of the same rights of privacy and self determination as enjoyed by those able to decide for themselves.[54] Some courts have sought to ensure the integrity of this process by insisting that the patient's wishes, expressed while competent, must be shown by 'clear and convincing' evidence so as to avoid life and death decisions made for another without firm and persuasive basis in fact.[20,21] Others have disagreed, finding this to be too heavy a burden of proof to impose.

Where the patient's wishes are unknown, most agree a 'best interests' test for decision-making is the best society has yet been able to devise. While imperfect, it does allow a choice to be exercised on behalf of the patient, rather than requiring that all treatment which helps to sustain life be continued – regardless of cost, inconvenience or prognosis – on the basis of not knowing what the patient would want. Most people want treatment that will help more than it will hurt, whose burdens are proportionate to its benefits. That is a reasonable goal. It seems fair for the family to apply it, in good faith and in consultation with the attending physicians, in deciding on care for an incapacitated loved one, whether newborn infant, child or adult.

These decisions should continue to be made by family and physicians as the norm.[55] They are intensely personal decisions and should remain private. The often cumbersome, costly and public scrutiny of the courts should not be invoked, save in the atypical case of disagreement, questioned motive, bad faith, bad practice, or where an affected party feels the need for court review.[56] The family, normally, is most qualified to make these decisions because of their affection for the patient, their knowledge of him, and their availability. At times, non-familial surrogates will most appropriately fulfill this role. Continuing the active role of the family in life and death decisions strengthens it and fosters the interdependence that is so valuable to society and to the sick and confused, who are some of its most vulnerable members.

Notes

1. In the U.K., see *Paton v. Trustees of the British Preg. Advisory Service* (1978) 2 All E.R. 987, C. v. S. [1988] QB 135; in the U.S., see *Planned Parenthood v. Danforth* 426 U.S. 52 (1976).

2. In the U.K., see *Gillick v. West Norfolk & Wisbech Area Health Auth.* (1985) 3 All E.R. 402 (HL); in the U.S., see *Akron v. Akron Center for Repro. Health* 103 S.Ct. 2481 (1983).
3. *Gillick*, note 2, *supra*; *Baird v. Attorney General* 360 N.E. 2d 288 (1977, Mass.).
4. Smith, *A Short Commentary on the Law of Scotland.* Edinburgh: W. Green & Son, Ltd., 1962, pp. 370–371.
5. *Bonner v. Moran* 126 F 2d 121 (1941, D.C. App.).
6. *Barber v. Superior Ct.* 147 Cal. App. 3d 1006 (1983).
7. *Guardianship of Grant* 747 Pac. 2d 445 (1987, Wash.).
8. *In Re Guardianship of Browning* 543 So. 2d 258 (1989, Fla. App.); *Re Hier* 464 N.E. 2d 959 (1984, Mass. App.); *Cobbs v. Grant* 8 Cal 3d 229 (1972).
9. *Cobbs*, note 8 *supra*, 8 Cal 3d at 244.
10. *Re Eichner* 420 N.E. 2d 64 (1981, NY).
11. See Kennedy, 'The Patient on the Clapham Omnibus'; 47 Mod. Law R. 454 (1984).
12. See *Salgo v. Leland Stanford Jr. Univ. Bd. of Trustees* 154 Cal App 2d 560 (1957); *Cobbs v. Grant*, note 8, *supra*.
13. *Young v. Oakland Gen. Hosp.* 437 N.W. 2d 321 (1989, Mich. App.); *Rasmussen v. Fleming* 741 Pac. 2d 674 (1987, Ariz.); *J.F.K. Mem. Hosp. v. Bludworth* 452 So. 2d 921 (1984, Fla.).
14. *Young v. Oakland Gen. Hosp.*, note 13 *supra*; *Pet. of Nemser* 273 N.Y.S. 2d 624 (1966, N.Y. App.).
15. See *Conservatorship of Drabick* 200 Cal. App. 3d 185 (1988); *Conservatorship of Morrison* 206 Cal. App. 3d 304 (1988).
16. *Schloendorff v. Society of New York Hosps.* 105 N.E. 92 (1914, N.Y.); *Sidaway v. Bethlem Royal Hosp. & Others* 2 W.L.R. 480 (HL) (1985); *Smith v. Auckland Hosp. Bd.* N.Z.L.R. 191 (1965).
17. *People v. Robbins* 443 N.Y.S. 2d 1016 (1981, N.Y. App.).
18. Report of the Pres. Comm. for the study of Ethical Problems in Medicine, *Deciding to Forego Life-Sustaining Treatment* Wash., D.C., U.S. Gov't. Print. Office, 1983, pp. 3–5, 132–3.
19. *Erickson v. Dilgard* 252 N.Y.S. 2d 705 (1962, N.Y. App.).
20. Compare *McConnell v. Beverly Enterprises—Connecticut, Inc.* 553 A. 2d 596 (1989, Conn.) (clear evidence), with *Re Westchester Co. Med. Ctr.* (O'Connor) 531 N.E. 2d 607 (1988, N.Y.) (evidence not clear).
21. *Cruzan v. Harmon* 760 S.W. 2d 408 (1988, Mo.), cert. granted 57 U.S.L.W. 3859 (1989, U.S.S.Ct.); Cruzan v. Director, Missouri Dept. of Health (U.S. Supreme Court, June 25th, 1990).
22. *Re Grady* 426 A. 2d 467 (1981, N.J.); *Guardianship of Eberhandy* 307 N.W. 2d 881 (1981, Wisc.).
23. *O'Connor*, note 20, *supra*; *Cruzan*, note 21, *supra*.
24. *In Re Guardianship of Browning* 543 So. 2d 258, 273 (1989, Fla. App.).
25. See, for example, Calif. Civil Code § 2430, *et. seq*.

26. *Canterbury v. Spence* 464 F. 2d 772 (1972, D.C. App.); *Gillick*, note 2, *supra*; [1987] 2 *Lancet*, 1474.
27. *Conservatorship of Waltz* 180 Cal. App. 3d 722 (1984).
28. *Matter of Spring* 399 N.E. 2d 493 (1979, Mass. App.); *Lydia E. Hall Hosp.* 455 N.Y.S. 2d 706 (1982, N.Y. App.).
29. *Matter of Sickewicz* 370 N.E. 2d 417 (1977, Mass.).
30. *Lane v. Candura* 376 N.E. 2d 1232 (1978, Mass. App.).
31. *Weber v. Stony Brook Hosp.* 456 N.E. 2d 1186 (1983, N.Y.), cert. den. 104 S. Ct. 560 (US).
32. See Meyers, 'Selective non-treatment of handicapped infants', in McLean (ed.), *Legal Issues in Human Reproduction* Aldershot: Gower, 1989, 113.
33. See *Bowen v. Amer. Hosp. Assn.* 106 S. Ct. 2101 (1986).
34. 45 C.F.R. 1340 (1985).
35. Mason & Meyers, 'Parental choice and selective non-treatment of deformed newborns: a view from mid-Atlantic', 12 *J. Med. Ethics* (1986), 67.
36. Duff & Campbell, 'Moral and Ethical Dilemmas in the Special-Care Nursing' 289 *N. Eng. J. Med.* 890 (1973).
37. Meyers, *The Human Body and the Law* Edinburgh: The Univ. Press, 1970 (1st Ed.), Chap. 6.
38. Duff, 'Guidelines for Deciding Care of Critically Ill or Dying' in *Bioethics* (3d ed., Shannon, ed.), p. 141.
39. See, for example, Calif. Civil Code §§ 34.7–34.10.
40. *Pierce v. Soc. of Sisters* 268 U.S. 510 (1925); *Prince v. Massachusetts* 321 U.S. 158 (1944).
41. *Hall v. State* 493 N.E. 2d 433 (1986, Ind.).
42. *Prince v. Mass.* 321 U.S. 158 (1944); *J.V. v. State* 516 So. 2d 1133 (1987, Fla. App.); *In Re Eric B.* 189 Cal. App. 3d 996 (1987).
43. *Re Hofbauer* 393 N.E. 2d 1009 (1979, N.Y.) (However, the parents agreed to consider conventional treatment if the child's condition worsened.)
44. *Re Phillip B* 92 Cal. App. 3d 796 (1979), cert. den. 100 S. Ct. 1597; but see *Guardianship of Phillip B* 139 Cal. App. 3d 407 (1983) (guardians authorized to consent to corrective surgery).
45. *Weber v. Stony Brook Hosp.* 456 N.E. 2d 1186 (1983, N.Y.), cert. den. 104 S. Ct. 560 (the infant would be paralyzed, bedridden, epileptic, severely retarded and only expected to survive up to 20 years with surgery).
46. *U.S. v. University Hosp.* 729 Fed. 2d 142 (1983).
47. *Joswick v. Lenox Hill Hosp.* 570 N.Y.S. 2d 803 (1986, N.Y. App.).
48. *Re Green* 92 A. 2d 387 (1972, Pa.).
49. *Re Hudson* 126 Pac. 2d 765 (1942, Wash.).
50. *Re Seiferth* 127 N.E. 2d 820 (1955, N.Y.).
51. *Re B* 497 S.W. 2d 831 (1973, Mo. App.).

52. *Wentzel v. Montgomery Gen. Hosp.* 447 A. 2d 124 (1982, Md.) cert. den. 103 S. Ct. 790.
53. *Re W.* 424 So. 2d 1015 (1982, La.).
54. *John F. Kennedy Mem. Hosp. v. Bludworth* 452 So. 2d 921 (1984, Fla.).
55. *In re Jobes* 529 A. 2d 434 (1987, N.J.).
56. *In re Barry* 445 So. 2d 365, 372 (1984, Fla. App.).

5. The family and contraception
Douglas Cusine

Recent concern over modern reproduction techniques has tended to eclipse the important legal issues surrounding those techniques which have precisely the opposite effect, namely, contraception, contragestion, and sterilization. These have been used for much longer than many of the modern reproductive techniques and yet here too, it is only in recent years that many issues have come before the UK courts. They have been asked to adjudicate upon contraception for those under the age of majority and the legality of sterilization for the mentally incompetent, both above and below the age of majority. It is these cases which will be my primary concern, but the use of the 'morning-after' pill and the drug RU486 (Mifepristone) have forced the medical and legal professions to consider carefully the precise effect of these devices in order to determine whether they are, or may be contraceptives, contragestives or abortifacients.

What is contraception?

At first sight, this may seem to be an odd question in that contraception is clearly something which is designed to prevent conception. However, as we shall see, 'conception' is defined in various ways which will not put lawyers at their ease because they prefer precise definitions which may make it easier to ascertain in which category a particular issue falls. 'Conception' is not legally defined and it should not be defined other than by the medical profession. However, there are a number of definitions, not all of which are consistent with each other. According to *Black's Medical Dictionary*, conception 'signifies the complex set of changes which occur in the ovum and in the body of the mother at the beginning of pregnancy. The precise moment of conception is that at which the male element or spermatozoon and the female element or ovum fuse together.' In other words, conception means fertilization. However, *Dorland's Medical Dictionary* defines the term as 'the onset of pregnancy, marked by implantation of the blastocyst'. In other words, conception is the same as implantation or nidation. In *The Oxford Dictionary of Medicine*, the following definition appears: 'The fertilization of an ovum by a spermatozoon and the implantation of the resulting zygote.'

The interesting point about the last definition is that it regards conception as a process and as such it covers the periods covered by the two other definitions. It is clear therefore, that no great assistance can be had from these conflicting definitions. However, at this point, perhaps one should ask; Is it important to define 'conception' and hence 'contraception' with the degree of precision to which lawyers are accustomed? In my opinion it is. If conception is not complete until implantation, then anything which happens thereafter falls within the realm of the law on abortion and thus only two terms are required. If on the other hand, conception is to be equated with fertilization, then there is an interval between that and implantation. That may have some significance in that there may be a fertilized egg, i.e. an embryo, or what is now in some quarters called a 'pre-embryo'.[1] The status of the pre-embryo is not an issue here, but it occupied the mind of the Warnock Committee[2] and the issue of the permissibility of research on embryos or pre-embryos has already been aired in Parliament in the discussion of the Human Fertilization and Embryology Bill. What is important for present purposes is the legality of devices which take effect after fertilization but before implantation. In this connection a new term has been spawned – contragestion.

Contragestion

The reason for the coining of this new term is the knowledge obtained from in vitro fertilization. It is now appreciated that fertilization of the human egg with human semen is not an event, but a process. After that process is complete, the fertilized egg has to travel up the Fallopian tube into the inter uterine cavity and thereafter it has to implant in the wall of the uterus (nidation), which, once again, is not an event, but a process. It may not implant but when it has, the woman is described as pregnant and so any device which interferes with that is an abortifacient. The term 'contragestion' which is short for contragestation was coined to describe the period between fertilization and implantation. That 'no-man's land' in the reproductive process may also be a legal 'no-man's land'. Contragestions have one or more of three effects, viz: – the function of the corpus luteum is disturbed, or tubal motility is affected, or ovo-implantation may be prevented.[3] In Scots law, before a person can be charged with carrying out an illegal abortion, it is necessary to establish that the woman was pregnant at the time.[4] English law, however, is bedevilled by section 59 of the Offences Against the Person Act 1861, which does not use the term 'abortion', but 'miscarriage'. There has been some controversy over this provision[5] but a great deal is to be said for the stance taken by the Attorney General who expressed the view that before there could be a miscarriage, there had to be carriage i.e. implantation.[6] Whether one accepts that view or not, it is clear that in Scotland, the use of devices in the intervening period between fertilization and implantation is not procuring an abortion.

It is useful at this point to consider very briefly some of the devices which may be used and to examine their effect in law. These are the intra-uterine device (IUD), post-coital pills (sometimes called post-coital contraceptives and in more common parlance the 'morning after' pill), anti-progesterones and anti-human chorionic gonadotrophin vaccines, menstrual extraction and RU 486.

The IUD

The IUD is usually inserted prior to intercourse, but the result is that any fertilized egg will not implant. However, an IUD may be fitted post-coitally and will have the same effect, but an IUD will also dislodge any embryos which have implanted prior to its being inserted. While that may amount to an abortion, it would probably be impossible for any prosecutor in Scotland to prove the existence of a pregnancy at the time. In England, somewhat illogically, it is submitted, it is possible to be convicted under the 1861 Act even although the woman is not pregnant, but the result is the same as that in Scotland in that the prosecutor has still to prove that the person thought that the woman was pregnant. In *R. v. Price*[7] a woman told her doctor that she was pregnant and that she wished to have an abortion. He told her that he did not believe that she was pregnant and advised that she should be fitted with an IUD. That was done and the woman, who was actually three and a half months pregnant, miscarried two days later. The doctor's conviction under the 1861 Act was quashed on the ground that there was insufficient evidence that the doctor believed that the woman was pregnant. Thus any doctor who inserts an IUD post-coitally will escape any criminal charges in Scotland and also in England. The belief in the possibility of a pregnancy would be irrelevant in Scotland since actual pregnancy has to be established and it would be insufficient in

The family and contraception

England on the basis of *Price*. In the Court of Appeal, Sachs LJ said that the essential issue for the jury was 'did the appellant... know or believe that the patient was pregnant and, accordingly, introduce the instrument with intent to produce a miscarriage'.[8] There was no question about whether the belief was reasonable or not, and it would appear that what is important is good faith and not that the belief be reasonable.[9]

Post-Coital Pills

The object of the so-called 'morning-after' pill is to prevent implantation after unprotected intercourse. What was said above in the context of IUDs, applies equally here.

Anti-Progesterones and Anti-HCG vaccines

Progesterone is a hormone essential for a pregnancy and without it, the lining of the uterus will not be capable of holding a fertilized egg. RU486 (Mifepristone), which is discussed later, will block the progesterone receptors in the uterus and so the fertilized egg will not implant: like an IUD, it will also dislodge any implanted embryos. In so far as it acts to prevent implantation, an anti-progesterone has the same legal implications as IUDs and post coital pills. In so far as it operates thereafter, it is an abortifacient, but then the issue of proof of pregnancy or a belief that the woman was pregnant is relevant.

Human chorionic gonadotrophin is a hormone produced by the developing embryo which is essential for implantation and the development of a vaccine (which is being funded by the World Health Organization)[10] will prevent implantation. The use of such a vaccine has the same legal implications as the pre-implantation use of anti-progesterones.

Menstrual Extraction

This is the method whereby the uterine contents are dislodged by suction around the expected time of menstruation. It is medically indicated when a woman is suffering from dysmenorrhoea (i.e. painful menstruation) but it may be used for birth control purposes and the removal of the uterine contents will prevent implantation or dislodge any implanted embryo. What has already been said, applies equally here also.

RU486

RU486 can also be used as a contraceptive and a contragestion, but it has caused greatest controversy because of its admitted use as an abortifacient. The prime legal difficulty lies in the ease with which it can be used: it does not involve either surgery, or anaesthesia, or a stay in hospital (no matter how short). The issue here is whether 'a registered medical practitioner remains in charge throughout'.[11]

Defining contraception is only the beginning of the problem. The next issue is to whom can contraception be made available, or, putting it another way, are there any restrictions on the provision of contraception to those who are usually regarded as being in special categories in the context of medical procedures, namely, those under the age of majority and the mentally handicapped.

Contraception for those under the age of majority: the Gillick[12] case and its implications

As Kennedy and Grubb have observed: 'Gillick shows how medical law is inseparably intertwined with medical ethics. It also shows you that as an area of law, medical law does not respect the traditional compartments with which lawyers have become familiar, such as torts, contracts, criminal law, family law and public law. Instead, medical law cuts across all of these subjects . . .'[13]

Gillick was concerned with three main issues. The first was whether a girl under the age of sixteen is able to consent to the provision of advice about contraception, and any concomitant examination and contraceptive provision. The second was what rights, if any, her parents have in respect of medical treatment on their child; and the third (which does not really touch upon our current theme) was whether a doctor is criminally liable if he provides contraceptive advice and/or treatment for a girl under sixteen without obtaining the consent of her parents.

The case went from the High Court (Woolf J., which decided against Mrs Gillick),[14] to the Court of Appeal (Parker, Eveleigh and Fox LJJ), which reversed the decision of Woolf J.,[15] and from there, to the House of Lords where a majority (Lords Fraser, Scarman and Bridge) decided against Mrs Gillick, the two other judges being Lords Templeman and Brandon.[16]

Legal capacity

The decision about the legal capacity of the girl under sixteen to give consent to medical treatment and in particular contraceptive advice

The family and contraception

turned on the interpretation of section 8 of the Family Law Reform Act 1969 the relevant parts of which are in the following terms:—

'(1) The consent of a minor who has obtained the age of sixteen years to any surgical, medical or dental treatment which, in the absence of consent, would constitute a trespass to his person, shall be as effective as it would be if he were of full age; and where a minor has by virtue of this section given an effective consent to that treatment it shall not be necessary to obtain any consent for it from his parent or guardian. . . .

(3) Nothing in this section shall be construed as making ineffective any consent which would have been effective if this section had not been enacted.'

Mrs Gillick contended that in any circumstances other than those envisaged by subsection (1), the consent of a minor would be ineffective and that subsection (3) left open the question whether the consent of someone under sixteen would have been effective in the absence of section 8(1). These arguments were rejected by the House of Lords which held, in effect, that subsection (1) was no more than declaratory and that subsection (3) was enacted for the avoidance of doubt.

Various other statutory provisions were mentioned in argument, but in the end of the day, Lord Fraser had this to say about them:—
'The statutory provisions to which I have referred do not differentiate so far as the capacity of a minor under sixteen is concerned between contraceptive advice and treatment and other forms of medical advice and treatment. It would, therefore, appear that, if the inference which Mrs Gillick's advisers seek to draw from the provisions is justified, a minor under the age of sixteen has no capacity to authorize any kind of medical treatment or examination of his own body. That seems to me so surprising that I cannot accept it in the absence of clear provisions to that effect. It seems to me verging on the absurd to suggest that a girl or boy aged fifteen could not effectively consent, for example, to have a medical examination of some trivial injury to his body or even to have a broken arm set. . . . Provided the patient . . . is capable of understanding what is proposed and of expressing his or her own wishes, I see no good reason for holding that he or she lacks the capacity to express them validly and effectively and to authorize the medical man to make the examination or give the treatment which he advises . . . On this part of the case accordingly I conclude that there is no statutory provision which compels me to

hold that a girl under the age of sixteen lacks the legal capacity to consent to contraceptive advice, examination and treatment provided that she has sufficient understanding and intelligence to know what they involve.'[17]

In Scots law, there is, as yet, no magic about the age sixteen; indeed it is an irrelevance in that the age of capacity is eighteen, but below that, there are two categories of persons who are under that age. The first is pupils who are boys under the age of fourteen and girls under the age of twelve. The other group are minors who are above these respective ages, but under eighteen.[18] These ages of twelve and fourteen are based on Roman law and are thought to represent the ages at which the Romans thought that girls and boys reached their respective ages of puberty. The other difference is that these ages are not laid down by statute, but rather as well-established at common law. While these are the ages at present, there is a proposal from the Scottish Law Commission to make the age sixteen in both cases and that proposal would include medical treatment. I shall return to these proposals. While the issue of consent to medical treatment has not been the subject of litigation in Scotland, it is submitted that in Scotland, the approach taken by Lord Fraser would find favour on the basis of contractual analogies: a minor, as a general rule, has the ability to enter into all the contracts which can be entered into by an adult, but must act with his curator's (guardian's) advice if he has one.[19] A minor, in Scotland, need not have a curator and hence may enter into contracts without the advice of an adult. Such minors are described as forisfamiliated and it would be absurd (to use Lord Fraser's words) to suggest that someone who may transact everyday business without the consent of an adult is not sufficiently mature to make decisions about his medical treatment.

Rights and Duties of Parents

Mrs Gillick asserted that she had an absolute right not only to be informed about, but also to veto the giving of contraceptive advice and treatment, but she accepted that these rights which she asserted were not for her benefit, but for those of her children. The point does not seem to have been made, but if Mrs Gillick's contention was sound it would follow that even if the doctor and the child thought that a particular course of action was in the child's best interests, that course of action could be vetoed by the parent. That must be a most doubtful proposition. Reference was made to a number of English cases of the last century dealing with custody,[20] but the House of Lords did not regard them as helpful in determining whether parents had the right to be informed about and the right of veto of medical treatment on a minor. Indeed, in a case in 1970, Lord Denning was firmly of the opinion that one of the cases which was referred to in *Gillick* reflected 'the attitude of a Victorian parent towards his children' and hence were, at best, unhelpful.[21] It would seem somewhat strange if a legal system, even one which places such reliance on precedent as English law does, could not throw off the fetters of cases decided against a social and moral background which bears no resemblance to that which obtains in society today. Fortunately, the House of Lords was not prepared to be manacled in this way. As Lord Scarman said, 'For reasons which I have endeavoured to develop, the case law of the nineteenth and earlier centuries is no guide to the application of the law in the conditions of today'.[22] On the specific point about parental rights, both he and Lord Fraser approved of the opinion expressed by Lord Denning that 'the legal right of a parent to the custody of a child ends at the eighteenth birthday; and even up till then, it is a dwindling right which the courts will hesitate to enforce against the wishes of the child, the older he is. It starts with a right of control and ends with little more than advice.'[23] Both Lord Scarman and Lord Fraser pointed out that Lord Denning was not the only judge to describe parental rights in the way that he did, but it is worthy of note that the comments made by other judges post-date Lord Denning's pronouncement which was made in 1970.

By contrast, the point made by Lord Denning was made in Scotland a century before by Lord Justice-Clerk Inglis in *Harvey* v. *Harvey*,[24] in which he enunciated the following principles: '(1) That the control to which a minor pubes is subjected does not proceed on any notion of his incapacity to exercise a rational judgement or choice, but rather arises, on the one hand, from a consideration of the reverence and obedience to parents which both the law of nature and the divine law enjoin, and, on the other hand, from a regard to the inexperience and immaturity of judgement on the part of the child, which require friendly and affectionate counsel and aid. (2) That the power of a father at this age is conferred not as a right of dominion, or even privilege for the father's own benefit or pleasure, but merely, or at least mainly, for the benefit, guidance and comfort of the child. (3) That, therefore, the father's authority and right of control may at this age be easily lost, either by an apparent intention to abandon it and leave the child to his own guidance, or by circumstances or conduct showing the father's inability or unwillingness to discharge rightly the parental duty towards his child. (4) That in all questions as to the loss of the parental control during puberty from any of these causes, the wishes and feelings of the child himself are entitled to a degree of weight corresponding to the amount of intelligence and right feeling which he may exhibit.'

It is important to observe that the Lord Justice-Clerk recognized that the minor might be entitled to express a view on any matter under consideration and that notion appears in the adoption legislation. In Scotland, a minor may object to an adoption order[25] and while a pupil has no such veto, the court must consider his views and those of a minor having regard to his age and understanding.[26] The other point worth noting is that the parent should be available for advice, a point also made in *Gillick*. Thomson argues, on the basis of the notion of custody, that the parent has a right to give the advice and it would follow that the child is under an obligation to consult the parent for that advice.[27] Objection may be made to this view. It seems strange to suggest that a child has a duty to seek advice, given that it may be clear that the child may not wish to follow the advice which would be given. Thomson says that if a girl consults her parents about contraception and they persuade her that contraception is not in her best interests, then no problem arises. He goes on to say, however, that if the parents fail to persuade her, that they cannot prevent her from obtaining contraceptives, 'unless it is clearly prejudicial to her interests to do so'.[28] It is not clear who makes the decision about those best interests, but Thomson would appear to mean the parents.

In *Gillick*, Lord Fraser required the doctor to be satisfied on that point,[29] but Lord Scarman did not require a 'best interests' test at all.[30] If, as has been suggested, both Scots and English law recognize the diminishing nature of parental rights, there seems to be no ground for imposing a duty on a child of sufficient maturity to seek advice and hence no basis for suggesting that the parents may have a right of veto. It is submitted that advice is something which is available if the person wishes to seek it. Someone who is recognized as being of sufficient maturity may decide whether to seek the advice of a parent or not. However, if Thomson is correct, another problem arises and it is that before a doctor could give contraceptive advice or treatment to, or perform any other medical procedure on a minor, he would have to know whether the parent(s) thought that this was in the child's best interests and it would also follow that if the parent(s) has a right of veto, then the doctor could not give the advice or provide any treatment even if he thought that that was in the child's best interests and he was satisfied that the child fully understood the implication of the treatment.

While it may be argued in any Scottish case in which the issues canvassed in *Gillick* have to be determined, that the views expressed by Lord Justice-Clerk Inglis were made against a social background which no longer obtains, it is submitted that they are consonant with those expressed in the House of Lords and are still valid. Norrie has argued most persuasively that the decision in *Gillick* has to be seen against a background of a legal system which differs so markedly from that in Scotland that it should be treated as a decision 'solely of relevance to English Law.'[31] While there is some force in that view, I feel that the opinions of the majority in *Gillick* are in keeping with the position at common law in Scotland and that it is unlikely that the Scottish courts would consider that dramatic changes took place at the age of twelve in girls and fourteen in boys. It can also be argued that in so far as Thomson's views are inconsistent with the views expressed by the majority in *Gillick*, they would not find favour in Scotland. However, the matter may never be put to the test because of the recommendations of the Scottish Law Commission.

The Scottish Law Commission proposals[32]

The Scottish Law Commission has now examined medical practice and has made recommendations for reform. It probably did not come as a surprise to anyone to be told that medical practice in Scotland generally mirrored the legal position in England. Why that should be is not clear, but in 1979, the Scottish Home and Health Department issued a circular which states that the age of consent for medical procedures is sixteen, and that where a medical procedure is proposed for someone under that age, the consent of the parents or guardians will be required, except in an emergency.[33] There is no legal basis for that, as the Commission points out,[34] but because there has not been any litigation on the matter in Scotland, there is some doubt about whether pupils i.e. those under twelve and fourteen respectively can give consent to medical procedures, provided they are capable of understanding its nature and implications, or whether the consent of parents would be required. The Commission say, rightly, that the consent of 'an older pupil child to simple treatment may well be legally effective'.[35] It would seem strange to suggest, for instance that a boy of thirteen who asks a doctor to remove something from his eye, cannot have that done without parental consent.

However, because of these uncertainties, the Commission produced a Consultative Memorandum[36] and held meetings in various places throughout Scotland in order to obtain the views of adults and children on their proposals.[37] 'Of all our provisional proposals for reform', the Commission observed, 'those concerning consent to medical treatment generated the largest response and most controversy.'[38]

The first area of concern was the age at which consent should be valid and whether there should be any exceptions. While there was general agreement on the age of sixteen, there was less agreement not on the need for exceptions, but on how they should be defined. In the end, the Commission opted for a recommendation, broadly reflecting that of Lord Scarman in *Gillick*[39] which is that a person under the age of sixteen should have the capacity to consent to medical procedures or treatment if the doctor is of the opinion that the young person is capable of understanding the nature and consequences of the treatment or procedure proposed. The Commission expressly rejected the view of Lord Fraser which was that in addition, the doctor must be of the opinion that the treatment or procedure was in the best interests of the patient. They also by implication rejected Thomson's view that parents have a right of veto if they do not consider the proposed action to be in the child's best interests.[40]

From what has been said, parents have little or no locus to object to a child being given contraceptive advice or treatment, or contragestives, or indeed any medical treatment or advice. In both Scotland and England, the doctor must be satisfied that someone under the age of consent is capable of understanding what is proposed and in Scotland, the younger the child is, the less likely it is that that understanding will be present. The requirement for understanding, of course, applies to all patients and all procedures and so a girl over the age of twelve, or a boy over the age of fourteen, while they may be of the age at which they can legally give consent, may lack the necessary understanding. The same can be said of someone over sixteen in England (and perhaps in the not too distant future, also in Scotland).

It would appear that in both England and Scotland, the parent may give advice, but only if asked, but, of course, it would be good medical practice for the doctor to ask a young person whether parental advice and guidance had been sought, especially in relation to contraception. Parental advice may be too late where it is contragestion which is being asked for. While it is unlikely that a child under the age of consent would seek sterilization, it is submitted that the situation is no different, but it is less likely that a doctor would agree to sterilize such a child. Lord Fraser would permit him to decline on the ground that it would not be in the child's best interests, but neither Lord Scarman nor the Scottish Law Commission consider that that test is relevant. There is, of course, nothing to prevent a doctor from refusing, but in order to bring himself within the test laid down by Lord Scarman and the Commission, he would have to say that he did not think that the child fully understood the implications. However, it is not entirely fanciful to say that a child of fifteen may fully understand sterilization and, if that were so, the doctor would be within the law to carry out the procedure and that without parental consent.

Sterilization of the mentally-handicapped

Problems of consent arise not only in relation to the young but also in relation to those who are, for some other reason, incapable of giving a valid consent to treatment. Here, too, the role of the family is an issue. It would, of course, be possible for the law to take the stance that because individuals cannot give consent, no-one may carry out any medical procedure without their consent, except in an emergency, or where there is a need for medical treatment for such individuals to alleviate, or treat the condition from which they suffer. Such medical procedures are governed by the Mental Health legislation.[41] There are, however, some situations in which other medical treatment or procedures may be thought desirable but where it is not directed at alleviating or treating their condition, but is indicated because of perceived undesirable consequences of not treating. In the United States, courts have been faced with the issue, for example, in connection with the treatment for the terminally ill mentally-handicapped patient,[42] and in relation to organ donation by the mentally handicapped.[43] The Scottish courts have not been faced with such problems, nor, until comparatively recently, had those in England.

One of the issues which those in medical practice have to consider on a fairly regular basis is whether to provide contraception for the mentally-handicapped in order to avoid pregnancy and birth for a patient who may be incapable of understanding either. Until recently, that would have been regarded as a legal 'grey area', and, while the English courts have not been asked to pronounce upon it, guidance can be had on the matter from the decisions on sterilization. Undoubtedly, if and when the Scottish courts are asked to consider either, the English cases will be regarded as highly persuasive and it is submitted that as the decisions are those of the House of Lords, it is unlikely that a Scottish court would depart from them.

In the last three years, the House of Lords has considered sterilization of the mentally-handicapped, both in adults and in those under the age of majority. These cases have arisen because of perceived risk of pregnancy to patients for whom contraception is not an available remedy. The use of contraceptives in the form of the pill requires some understanding of when the pills have to be taken. Because of that, for many patients, that form of contraception would be inappropriate. Even if the patient could understand that form of contraception, it might not be suitable because of the use of other medication, and the side effects of the pill. IUDs may become dislodged and a patient may not be able to explain discomfort to the doctor to enable remedial measures to be taken in time. In any such case, the only method of ensuring complete protection is sterilization. It is quite clear from the reported cases that the courts will, in certain circumstances, permit sterilization of the mentally-handicapped.

However, as we shall see, the approach to the sterilization on those under the age of majority may be different from that to be taken when the person is of full age. (It is interesting to note in passing that all of the sterilization cases in this country and those which have been referred to by the English courts have involved the sterilization of females.)

In the first case before the House of Lords,[44] the person on whose behalf a decision was sought was a seventeen-year-old girl (Janette). She was mentally-handicapped with the intelligence level of a girl of five; she was also epileptic. However, she had shown signs that she was, in the words of the Lord Chancellor 'vulnerable to sexual approaches'[45] and there was a danger of pregnancy resulting from casual sexual intercourse. The local borough council in whose care she was was supported by Janette's mother in an application to the High Court for wardship so that Janette could be sterilized. The High Court granted the permission for the sterilization and that decision was upheld both by the Court of Appeal and by the House of Lords. The only previous decision is that of Heilbron J. in *Re. D (A minor)*[46] where the judge was asked to authorize the sterilization of an eleven-year-old girl who suffered from Sotos' Syndrome which left her mentally impaired and emotionally unstable. While she would always be mentally impaired, there was evidence that her condition might improve and improve to the extent that she might be able to make the decision for herself. While Heilbron J. was in no doubt about the court's power to grant the necessary authority, she did not grant it because of the prognosis. The decision had to be reached by determining what was in the child's best interests and they dictated that the decision should be against sterilization at that point. In *Re B*, Janette would not improve, she would not understand the consequences of unprotected sexual intercourse and would never realize that she had lost the power to reproduce, if the sterilization went ahead. All three courts emphasized the need for the decision to be reached by considering only Janette's best interests. There was evidence that the alternatives – contraception in its various forms were, for a variety of reasons unsuitable or would be ineffective and accordingly, sterilization was the only method of protecting Janette from pregnancy. It was in her interests to be so protected because 'pregnancy would be an unmitigated disaster'.[47]

In reaching that decision, the court considered two arguments, one of which recommended itself to the Supreme Court of Canada in a similar case – *Re Eve*.[48] That argument was that while sterilization might be carried out for therapeutic reasons, it could never be justified if the grounds were non-therapeutic. However, it was shown in *Re Eve* that a pregnancy for her would not be any more difficult than for any other woman and the only additional factor was the anxiety caused to Eve's mother. In the circumstances, the Supreme Court of Canada rejected the request for sterilization and the sterilization was in the circumstances described as 'non-therapeutic'. It may be that what the English courts described as being in the best interests would correspond with what the court in Canada described as therapeutic and vice-versa and so the difference is one of semantics rather than substance. However, 'non-therapeutic' has a well-understood meaning in medical parlance and for that reason, it was confusing to use it in a court case as meaning the same as 'in the best interests' if indeed that was what was meant. While the House of Lords may have misinterpreted the significance of the use of the term 'non-therapeutic' in the Canadian case, they disapproved of the limitation of sterilization of the mentally-handicapped to cases where there were therapeutic grounds.[49]

The other argument which was rejected was that everyone has a fundamental right to reproduce, as is recognized in Article 12 of the European Convention on Human Rights. In the opinion of the Lord Chancellor, there is no such right where the individual is incapable of understanding the link between sexual intercourse and pregnancy and birth[50] and Lord Oliver also dismissed this argument, albeit on slightly different grounds.[51]

Thus the House of Lords unanimously approved the sterilization as being in the child's best interests. Only Lord Templeman, however, expressly made the point that sterilization of those under majority should be carried out only with the permission of the High Court. 'A court exercising the wardship jurisdiction emanating from the Crown is the only authority which is empowered to authorize such a drastic step as sterilization after a full and informal investigation.'[52] There is no doubt that such a court should act as 'a wise and prudent parent'[53] would act and the comments made by Lord Templeman have been criticized on the basis that parents should be able themselves to make such decisions.[54] That criticism is misplaced, in that in both the English case *Re D* and the Canadian case *Re Eve*, the decision was against sterilization, and there was evidence in both cases the parents saw sterilization as being in the best interests of their children. It is therefore important that the role of the courts is preserved to ensure that it is the best interests of the child which are considered and in many instances, the parents will not be the best persons to make that decision because their interests are inextricably intertwined with those of the child.

In *Re Eve*, the court was dealing with an adult and it commented upon the disappearance of the *parens patriae* power, a right to make decisions about the welfare of adult incompetents, previously invested in judges and derived from the Crown.[55] That problem which not arising in *Re B* did arise in *F v. West Berkshire Health Authority*,[56] the second case decided in the House of Lords, this time about sterilization of an adult who was mentally handicapped.

The facts in *F* were, briefly, that the woman was thirty-six years of age, but with serious mental disability and she was a voluntary inpatient at a mental hospital. She had formed a sexual relationship with another patient and once again, it was regarded as being disastrous for her if she became pregnant. As in *Re B*, contraception was not a viable alternative. Her mother sought a declaration from the High Court that the fact that F. could not give consent to a sterilization would not make that operation unlawful. It was conceded by the court that the *parens patriae* jurisdiction had disappeared as the result of the passing of the Mental Health Acts, but nevertheless, the court gave the necessary ruling. On appeal, both the Court of Appeal and the House of Lords upheld that decision.

Many of the arguments which were advanced before the court in *Re. B* were reiterated in *F*, but the court was unanimous in the opinion that a sterilization can be carried out if it is in the best interests of the patient. For Lords Brandon and Goff, the doctor not only could act on behalf of those who are incapable of giving consent, such action could be regarded as justified by the doctrine of necessity or emergency and hence there would be a duty to act.[57] However, although in *Re. B* at least for Lord Templeman, the decision had to be taken by the High Court, in *F.*, the court pointed out that the test of whether the proposed sterilization was in the best interests of the patient, a decision could be reached by applying the traditional test namely, whether a respectable body of medical opinion would accept the treatment as the appropriate treatment at the time. While the majority of the judges took the view that a decision of the court was not necessary, they did consider that it was desirable to seek the court's views. However, Lord Griffiths, echoing the views of Lord Templeman, thought that a decision had to be made by the court.[58]

In Scotland, the courts have not yet had to consider either of these problems. Wardship does not exist, but traditionally, the courts have exercised control over the exercise of parental authority in the interests of the children.[59] If the courts in Scotland were to follow the approach taken by the House of Lords in *Re B*, in my opinion, the courts would have no difficulty in exercising jurisdiction over a mentally-handicapped child where there was a proposal to carry out a sterilization. Even if it were argued that the test is what is in the child's best interests and that a sterilization cannot be in the child's best interests, there is authority, albeit in a different context (of blood tests) for carrying out a blood test where that would not be against the interests of the child.[60] On that basis, there is nothing to prevent the courts authorizing a sterilization in circumstances such as those in *Re. B*.

Sterilization on mentally-handicapped adults presents less of a problem in Scotland. In England, the jurisdiction *parens patriae* was abolished, but was not replaced. In Scotland, under the Mental Deficiency and Lunacy (Scotland) Act 1913 a guardian appointed thereunder had the same powers as a father has in relation to his pupil child. While there might have been some doubt about whether that power would have extended to sterilization of a mentally-handicapped adult, the statute was repealed by the Mental Health Acts. However, as has been shown recently, the common law power to appoint a tutor-dative is still extant,[61] and so a tutor-dative, if appointed could seek the court's authority for sterilization. It remains to be seen whether the Scottish courts would follow the majority view of the judges in *F.* – that an application to the courts while desirable, is not essential – or whether they would follow both Lord Templeman in *Re B* and Lord Griffiths in *F* and require a decision by the courts. In my opinion, the Scottish courts would take the latter course.

As was said earlier, the Scottish courts have, for a considerable period, recognized that parental power is a power which declines with the age of the child and would therefore consider children under the age of majority as being in law capable of making decisions about contraception, contragestion and sterilization. Whether a particular child would be provided with any of these would in each case be determined by the ability of the child to understand the nature of the procedure and the risks. My view is that while the parents may give advice, if it is sought, they have no power of veto. In the equally-controversial area of sterilization of the mentally-handicapped, the decision in the case of the child is one which has to be reached by considering what is in the interests of the child and not what is in the interests of the parents. Once again, the parents do not have the right to decide, nor would they have a right of veto.

Where the person is an adult, the basis for the decision is the same. While the views of parents, or in this case, those of other members of the family in the absence of parents may be persuasive, the ultimate decision may be one solely for the doctors, or perhaps one for the court. While it is perhaps unlikely in Scotland, where these sterilization cases have still to be decided by the courts, that doctors would carry out a sterilization of a person without the consent of the parents of a mentally-handicapped child, nor carry out a sterilization against their wishes, there seems to be little doubt from the English cases, that in the first case, they do not need the consent and in the second, they may ignore the refusal to give consent. The same would apply where there was a parent of an adult person who was mentally-handicapped. In such a case, proxy consent makes no sense and the justification for sterilization must lie elsewhere. So far as the patient's best interests are concerned, these are for the patient to determine, except for Lord

Fraser who in *Gillick* required the doctor to be satisfied that contraception was in the best interests of the patient where the patient is under sixteen. In the case of the mentally-handicapped, the decision about treatment for them, other than treatment under the Mental Health legislation, is based entirely on what is in their best interests; in the case of those under the age of majority or whom sterilization is recommended, the decision may be one for the courts, as Lord Templeman said in *Re B*, but in the case of adults, the doctors may decide; but there is a clear recommendation from the House of Lords that all sterilizations should be decided upon by the court.

Notes

1. This is the term which is now used by the Interim (formerly the Voluntary) Licensing Authority.
2. Report of the Committee of Inquiry into Human Fertilisation and Embryology London: HMSO, Cmnd 9314 (1984).
3. Board 'Endometrial carbonic anhydrase after diethylstilbestrol as a post coital anti-fertility agent' 36 *Obst. & Gynae* (1970) 347–349; Van Santen & Haspels 'Interfering with implantation by post-coital oestrogen administration' 7 *Proc. Reprod. Biol.* (1980) 310–323.
4. *HMA v. Semple* 1937 JC 41.
5. See for example Mason & McCall Smith op. cit. ch 5; Mason *Human Life and Medical Practice* ch. 7; Mason 'Abortion and the Law' in Mclean (ed) *Legal Issues in Human Reproduction*, Aldershot: Gower, 1988, ch. 3; Keown *Abortion, Doctors and the Law* Cambridge: Cambridge University Press, 1988; Kennedy and Grubb *Medical Law: Text and Materials* London: Butterworths, 1989 ch. 9.
6. H.C. Deb. Vol. 42 cols. 238–239 (11 May 1983).
7. [1968] 2 All ER. 282.
8. Note 7, *supra*, at p. 283.
9. *R. v. Smith* [1974] 1 All ER. 276.
10. 'WHO Task Force on Postovulatory Methods for Fertility Regulation' 4 *Human Reproduction* (1989) 718.
11. *Royal College of Nursing v. DHSS* [1981] AC 800, per Lord Diplock at 828–829.
12. [1985] 3 All ER. 402.
13. p. 3.
14. [1984] 1 All ER. 365.
15. [1985] 1 All ER. 533.
16. [1985] 3 All ER. 402.
17. Note 16, *supra*, at p. 409.
18. Ersk. Inst. 1, 7, 14.

19. Gloag on Contract 2nd ed. 79—81.
20. Note 19, *supra*, per Lord Fraser at p. 411—412.
21. *Hewer v. Bryant* [1969] 3 All ER. 578 at 582.
22. Note 19, *supra*, at p. 412.
23. *Hewer supra* at 582.
24. (1860) 22 D. 1198 at 1208.
25. Adoption (Scotland) Act 1978 s. 12(8).
26. *ibid*., s. 6.
27. *Family Law in Scotland* Edinburgh: Butterworths, 1987, p. 171.
28. *ibid*.
29. N. 19, *supra*, at p. 412—413.
30. N. 19, *supra*, at p. 424.
31. 'The Gillick Case and Parental Rights in Scots Law' 1985 Scots Law Times (News) 157—162 at 162.
32. Report on the Legal Capacity and Responsibility of Minors and Pupils (Scot. Law Com. No. 110) 1987.
33. Circular SHHD (DS(79)2), January 1979.
34. *ibid*., para. 2.9.
35. *ibid*., para. 2.9.
36. Legal Capacity and Responsibility of Minors and Pupils Consultative Memo. No. 65, June 1985.
37. Report para. 1.2.
38. *ibid*., para. 3.61.
39. *ibid*., para. 3.93.
40. *ibid*., paras. 3.77—3.82.
41. Mental Health (Scotland) Act 1984.
42. *Superintendent of Belchertown State School v. Saikewicz* 370 NE 2d 417 (1976, Mass.).
43. *Strunk v. Strunk* 445 SW 2d 145 (1969, Ky.).
44. [1987] 2 All ER. 206.
45. *ibid*., at p. 212.
46. [1976] 1 All ER. 326.
47. [1987] 2 All ER. at 214.
48. (1986) 2 SCR 388.
49. N. 19, *supra*. For example, Lord Hailsham at p. 213; Lord Bridge at p. 214; Lord Oliver at p. 219.
50. [1987] 2 All ER. at p. 213.
51. *ibid*., per Lord Oliver at p. 219.
52. *ibid*., at p. 217.
53. *R v Gyngall* [1893] 2 QB 232, per Lord Esher MR. at p. 241.
54. Grubb and Pearl, 'Sterilisation and the Courts' *Cambridge Law Journal* (1987) pp. 439—464.
55. The disappearance of this jurisdiction was regretted by Wood J. in *T v. T* [1988] 1 All ER. 613.
56. [1989] 2 All ER. 545.
57. N. 19, *supra*; Lord Brandon at pp. 551—552; Lord Goff at pp. 566—567.

58. *ibid.*, at pp. 561–562.
59. Fraser on *Parent and Child* 3rd ed p. 89.
60. *Docherty v. McGlynn* 1985 Scots Law Times, 237.
61. Ward, 'Revival of Tutors Dative' 1987 Scots Law Times (News) 69.

6. Regulating pregnancy: should we and can we?
Elaine Sutherland

The importance of the ante-natal environment for the development of the fetus and, ultimately, the neonate and child is now accepted as being considerable. This is acknowledged in many jurisdictions by the provision of special, and often free, health care and other benefits for pregnant women. Further recognition is found in the civil and criminal liability attaching to third parties who cause injury to the fetus.

Despite earlier examples of rejection of the principle,[1] many jurisdictions now accept that, where a third party negligently causes injury to the fetus and there is a subsequent live birth, the third party will be liable in delict or tort. In Canada, such liability was accepted as early as 1933.[2] Reviewing the current state of the law in Scotland in 1973, the Scottish Law Commission concluded that, despite the lack of express judicial decision on the point, the general principles of delictual liability applied and no legislation was required in order to permit recovery in such circumstances.[3] In England and Wales, the position was reviewed in 1974 and, while academic opinion supported the existence of liability,[4] it was felt that legislation was necessary for clarification.[5] The Congenital Disabilities (Civil Liability) Act followed the Law Commission's recommendations in providing that, where the child was subsequently born alive, a third party whose negligence caused injury to that child would be liable in damages to the child despite the fact that the negligence predated the child's birth.[6] Initially, liability was rejected in the USA for a number of reasons including: a lack of precedent; the view of the fetus as part of the mother, with no independent existence and thus, no independent right of action; the view that this was a matter for the legislature and not the courts; and the difficulty of proving causation.[7] However, opinion changed and, from the 1940s onwards the earlier decisions were overruled and tort liability for ante-natal injury is now well established.[8]

There is a scarcity of common law authority on criminal liability for ante-natal injury. Judicial decisions here are concerned largely with the interpretation of statute and, in particular, whether or not the word 'person' could include a fetus. Certainly, one case from the USA supports the view that the fetus must live outside the womb for

Regulating pregnancy: should we and can we?

a period of time before a murder charge could be relevant.[9] In that case, it was alleged that, in the course of attacking his estranged wife, the accused caused the death of the fetus she was carrying and that it was later surgically removed. The court took the view that while the accused might be guilty of a number of other offences, including criminal abortion, he could not be guilty of murder. Where the fetus does survive the birth, there is authority from both Scotland[10] and the USA[11] to support the view that the fact that the injury which caused death was sustained *in utero*, will not help the accused to escape criminal responsibility. However, a recent English case denied the fetus the status of a 'person' where the making of a threat to harm that person would have been an offence.[12]

While the question of third party liability for antenatal injury is well established, one particular 'third party' is in a special position. The carrier of the fetus, who will usually also be the biological mother,[13] is in a unique position to control the ante-natal environment. The attention she pays to her own physical health and the risks to which she subjects her own body may have a direct impact on the well-being of the fetus and, ultimately, the child subsequently born. Courts have recognized this in attaching importance to antenatal conduct when considering whether or not a child has been subject to neglect in the past, and have taken the view that babies who were born suffering from withdrawal symptoms from drugs were *prima facie* showing signs of neglect.[14] It is submitted that every child has the right to start life in the best state of health possible in the circumstances. If this proposition is accepted, the question arises of whether or not it is legitimate for society to intervene in order to encourage and, if necessary, to compel pregnant women to follow a regime of conduct which will protect the fetus from certain risks or even to provide the optimal environment for the fetus. If the case for some kind of intervention is accepted, the types of intervention which are appropriate and the circumstances in which they are warranted must then be identified.

Sources of possible harm

Antenatal injury resulting in harm to the child subsequently born can originate in two distinct ways. These can be described as 'pre-conception' and 'post-conception'. In the context of the pre-conception situation, the harm results where the woman conceives in the knowledge that there is a risk that the child will suffer from a particular undesirable condition. Examples here include cases where she knows herself to be HIV positive or where, as a result of genetic counselling, she has been warned that there is a risk that the child will suffer from a particular genetically transmitted disease. Indeed, where there is a family history of a particular disease and the woman does not seek genetic counselling, she might be accused of showing a negligent disregard for the possibility of transmitting the disease. It is acknowledged that the same problem may arise where a father ignores similar conditions in respect of himself, but it is with maternal responsibility that we are concerned here.

Post-conception antenatal injury may result from a variety of forms of behaviour by the mother. Perhaps the most widely publicized is the consumption by the pregnant woman of a variety of drugs including, cocaine, heroin, amphetamines, barbiturates, tobacco and alcohol.[15] In addition, a number of drugs, appropriately prescribed by a physician, may have an adverse effect on the fetus.[16] Other conduct, such as participation in a particular sport or continuing in certain types of employment may also present a risk. Nor need the pregnant woman's behaviour be active. Simply by failing to take care of her own health or to seek proper antenatal care she may be putting the fetus at risk. Furthermore, the woman's conduct is not always a sign of a callous disregard for the fetus' welfare. Economic circumstances may dictate the continuation of a particular form of employment or preclude an ideal physical or dietary regime. The woman's decision may be attributable to her moral or religious beliefs. Refusal of a blood transfusion or a caesarian delivery may be prompted by the best of motives, as the woman perceives them. As for the alcoholic or drug addict, to suggest that a free choice is made as to behaviour in these cases is at best, naïve.

The distinction between pre- and post-conception injury is of considerable significance. For the woman herself, the former situation presents the choice between having or not having a child. In the post-conception context, the women need only consider altering her behaviour in the short term, in most cases. Where medical intervention is involved, the intrusion – be it physical, moral or religious – is more dramatic. For society, the distinction is relevant to the issue of what, if any, form of intervention is legitimate in each context. The question of intervention in the post-conception context will be addressed presently. At this point, it is appropriate to consider the question of intervention in the pre-conception context.

Where the risk of injury to the child can be ascribed to a pre-existing condition the question is largely whether or not a woman

Regulating pregnancy: should we and can we?

should decide to procreate in the face of that knowledge. The choice may not be absolute. In some circumstances, a woman could conceive, undergo tests and, on the basis of the finding on whether or not a genetic condition has been transmitted, decide to proceed with or to terminate the pregnancy. Clearly, this option would be unacceptable to many women and, in any event, it does not deal with the situation where the harm is unavoidable. It should be stressed that all that has been considered so far is the choice facing the particular woman. It is not suggested that society has any right to prevent individuals from having children. Quite apart from the fact that such a notion produces abhorrence at the level of 'gut reaction' and raises the terrifying spectre of selective reproduction, it would fall foul of the European Convention on Human Rights and Fundamental Freedoms.[17] However, it is appropriate to consider whether or not any child born with an injury which resulted from a pre-conception risk should be able to recover damages from a mother who knew of that risk.

The issue is, as yet, unlitigated. However, assistance may be found in the development of the cases in the USA, dealing with third party liability in what have become known as the 'wrongful life' cases. Where a physician knew of or ought to have advised testing for the possibility that the child would suffer from a particular disease or disability and failed to inform the parents of this, the child subsequently being born with the condition, the courts were initially unwilling to permit either the parents or the child to recover damages for the physician's negligence. Examples of the courts' refusal to permit recovery include cases where: there was a failure to warn of the risks where a woman had been exposed to reubella;[18] failure to test for neurofibromatosis, despite evidence of the condition in the child's siblings;[19] and failure to offer amniocentesis to a pregnant woman in her late thirties, where the woman subsequently gave birth to a child suffering from Down's syndrome.[20] The refusal to permit recovery was based on a lack of precedent, and the view that public policy required the courts to regard life, even with severe disability, as better than no life at all. Inroads on the courts' position began when parents were allowed to recover damages on the basis that there was a public interest in ensuring that medical testing was carried out with all due skill and care.[21] Finally, the child's right to recover damages was accepted in *Curlender v Bio-Science Laboratories*.[22] There, the parents underwent tests to reveal their status as carriers of Tay-Sachs disease. It was alleged that the tests were negligently carried out and, as a result, the wife gave birth to a child suffering from the disease. In holding competent the child's claim for damages for pain and suffering and for the additional costs of care, based on the child's actual, rather than an actuarial, life expectancy, and in finding punitive damages competent, the court reviewed the previous decisions and concluded that where there was a breach of a duty of care, a legally recognizable wrong had been committed and that public policy required that a remedy should be provided in such circumstances. The court's reasoning has been followed in subsequent cases.[23]

Development of this area of the law in the UK has so far been confined to acknowledging the parents' right to claim damages in cases of failed sterilizations and vasectomies.[24] The only reported case to date where a child claimed damages involved the failure of a physician to advise the mother, who had been exposed to rubella during pregnancy, of the possible consequences.[25] The child's claim was rejected on much the same reasoning as the earlier American cases.

Where, then, does this leave the woman who decides to have a child, despite warnings that there is substantial risk that the child will suffer from a particular disease or condition? Could and should she be held liable to the child in damages? The court in *Curlender* considered the fear that such actions might be raised and dismissed the fear as 'groundless'.[26] It is submitted that they may have been too hasty in reaching this conclusion since, as the law in the USA stands, the liability applicable to a third party could very well be extended to the mother. It might be argued that such liability effectively penalizes the woman for her decision to have a child and, as such, would be unconstitutional in the USA.[27] It might also constitute a breach of the European Convention on Human Rights.[28] Whether or not the mother should be so liable raises the question of whether or not mothers, by virtue of their special relationship with the fetus, should be granted immunity from liability. The same issue arises in the context of the mother's liability in delict or tort where the injury is sustained by the child after conception and are discussed below.

The case against intervention in the post-conception context

Clearly, views on the acceptability or otherwise of intervention will vary depending on the type of intervention proposed and the degree of intrusion attached to it. However, there are some general arguments against intervention which should be addressed.

First, it can be argued that intervention is an intrusion on the rights

Regulating pregnancy: should we and can we?

of women to freedom of choice and privacy. By regulating the antenatal environment, society would gain considerable control over the lives and bodies of pregnant women.[29] It would be yet another example of defining women's role in society in terms of the ability to carry and bear children. Given the hard-won gains in the USA[30] and, to some extent, in the UK,[31] in terms of a degree of autonomy achieved by women in the context of abortion, it is anomalous that there should be this new intrusion. Indeed, some would see the support for intervention as a backdoor attack on a woman's right to choose to have an abortion. Polarizing opinion as it does, the abortion question should be considered at this point, lest it cloud discussion of the other issues. Freedom to choose abortion need not be inconsistent with setting certain standards for the antenatal regime. A woman can have the right to choose abortion and it is only once she has decided not to exercise this option; that is to say, once she has decided to proceed with the pregnancy; that she acquires responsibilities in respect of the fetus' well-being. Thus, freedom of choice in the context of abortion need not be compromised by regulation of the antenatal environment.

Nonetheless, regulation of the antenatal regime would impose restrictions on a pregnant woman's freedom. Prohibiting the sale of tobacco and alcohol to pregnant women would be an albeit impractical possibility here. To deny pregnant women access to non-prescription drugs such as heroin or cocaine could hardly be described as a restriction, since the use of them is usually illegal anyway. However, were special measures, such as detention, to be used in order to enforce the prohibition in the case of pregnant women, the degree of intrusion would certainly be increased. Were certain kinds of employment to be barred to pregnant women, the economic impact on these women could be severe, but this could be offset by adequate compensation from the state. Perhaps the most dramatic example of intrusion is court-ordered medical or surgical treatment: for example, a blood transfusion or a caesarian delivery.

The question then is, can this intrusion on the free choice of women ever be justified? It is submitted that it can. Where a woman decides to proceed with her pregnancy, it is foreseeable that her conduct could affect the fetus. Her responsibility to avoid causing harm is simply another example of the duty which all persons owe not to cause harm to others. That this may involve restrictions to which other members of the community are not subject is an unavoidable consequence of the particular circumstances of the case.

In any event, restrictions will usually be temporary and of relatively short duration. This is not a cry for wholesale, sweeping regulation of the antenatal regime, and the kinds of intervention which may be justified and the circumstances in which they might be appropriate are discussed below.

A second objection to intervention is that it would disrupt family harmony and might create future resentment on the part of the mother towards the child. Since the ultimate goal of intervention would be to prevent harm from occurring, it can be seen as reducing the disruption of family life and, thereby, family harmony. Where the intervention takes place after the harm has occurred, the potentially resentful mother may indeed be caring for the disabled child. The only parallel here arises where a child is empowered to sue a parent for injury sustained after birth: for example; in a car accident. There is no evidence to suggest that resentment results in this context. However, were a mother to show signs of resentment towards a child who had recovered damages for her negligent antenatal conduct, this might be evidence that she was not the best person to care for the child.

A third objection to intervention is that, in order to avoid intrusion in her life, a woman might seek to terminate her pregnancy. This would only apply where the form of intervention was quite radical. Nonetheless, it has to be admitted that, were a heroin addict to face detention in order to prevent her from having access to the drug, she might find abortion a preferable alternative.

Further objections to intervention suggest that the availability of civil actions might be misused by an aggrieved husband in matrimonial disputes or that such right of action would be pointless, since most mothers would not be able to pay any damages awarded. In answer, it can be said that the courts rarely look at the motives of litigants pursuing legitimate legal claims and that the defender's inability to pay has never been a consideration in making awards of damages.

The above suggests that complete opposition to some degree of intervention is unwarranted. What then, are the arguments in favour of some degree of intervention?

The case for intervention in the post-conception context

One might be accused of stating the obvious by suggesting that it is in the interests of every child that he or she should be born in as healthy a condition as is possible in the circumstances. Clearly, it is unavoidable that some children will be born with health problems and that these problems will be of varying severity. However, where it is possible to avoid injury, it is in the child's interest that the injury should be avoided. Again, to state the obvious, neither a child nor a fetus is in any position to protect this interest. Society has no hesitation in taking upon itself, at least in theory, the duty to protect children and it can be argued that it is simply anticipating that duty when it seeks to protect a fetus that will become a child. Furthermore, it is in the interests of society to ensure that its members are as healthy as possible in order to afford those members every opportunity to participate in and to contribute to that society. In pursuit of its own and the individual's interests it is not accepted that society should be permitted to take any steps, regardless of their severity.

A good example of limitation on intervention can be seen in the context of child protection, where the legislation acknowledges that the protection of the child's interests must be conducted within a specified framework. While a host of powers are delegated to specific agencies, including: the investigation of a particular family's lifestyle, the supervision of parenting, and the temporary or permanent removal of the child from the family's home, these powers may only be exercised in line with procedures aimed at protecting family privacy, ensuring that allegations are supported by sufficient evidence, affording all interested parties the opportunity to be heard, and requiring those who make decisions to give reasons for them. Once intervention in the conduct of a pregnant woman is placed within a system requiring a similar set of safeguards, it is submitted that it becomes considerably less threatening.

Nor is there anything new in the law having regard to the antenatal situation, provided that a live child is born subsequently. As has already been illustrated, a third party can be liable in delict and tort for injury to a child despite the fact that the delictual or tortuous act predated the child's birth.[32] Similarly, the criminal law will not usually regard it as a defence for the accused to argue that the alleged criminal conduct took place before the child was born.[33] Again, in assessing whether or not a child has been neglected or abused in the past, courts are showing an increasing willingness to view the antenatal situation as part of the continuum of child care.[34] There are other examples of the law's willingness to accord benefits to a child where these are derived from a time prior to the child's birth. In many jurisdictions, a posthumous child has the same succession rights as a child who was alive at the time of the parent's death.[35] Similarly, the child's right to claim damages for the loss of a parent is often extended to the posthumous child.[36]

As will be argued later, to hold the mother liable in delict or tort is no departure from the general principles applying in many other areas of the law.[37] To regulate the antenatal environment in other ways may, at first sight, appear to be a departure from established legal principle. However, there is nothing new in attempting to prevent a harm which, if not avoided, would entitle the injured party to compensation.

For example, a person who has been knocked down and injured in a road accident will be entitled to compensation if he or she can show that there was some fault or negligence on the part of the driver of the offending car. But the legal system does not leave it at that. In order to prevent accidents, a number of requirements exist including: requiring potential drivers to pass a test, demonstrating certain minimum standards of competence, before they are permitted to drive alone; requiring qualified drivers to notify the authorities if they develop certain medical conditions, such as epilepsy; providing maximum acceptable levels of alcohol content in the body of the driver; laying down maximum speed limits; and penalizing drivers who drive in particular ways and thereby breach the rules of acceptable road conduct. All of these requirements are aimed at preventing accidents from occurring. Of course, the legal system could do more. It could require every driver to submit to an annual medical examination and test of driving proficiency. This is not done because the cost, inconvenience, and invasion of privacy would outweigh the benefit in terms of a reduction in the number of accidents.

The parallel with regulation of the antenatal environment here is clear. Attempting to avoid harm to the fetus, rather than simply compensating for it, is not a radically new form of social control. However, the content of any such regulation would have to be justified when weighed against other factors such as effectiveness and the degree of intrusion on the rights of others. Possible types of intervention and how they meet this test will now be considered.

Possible types of intervention

A number of possible forms of intervention are discussed below. Some can be described as solely preventative, while others involve a degree of deterrence or punishment. All except the first involve some element of intrusion on the freedom of action of the pregnant woman.

The first, and least invasive, form of intervention is already in existence in what might be described as the 'affluent western world'. This involves the state in providing health education, free antenatal care and, in some cases, additional financial support, for pregnant women. Where this is available to the woman on a voluntary basis, it can hardly be described as any restriction on women's freedom, unless one views the social pressure which supports participation as compelling individuals to do so against their will. Indeed, greater funding of programmes of this kind could improve the lifestyle of many women.

However, were participation in the educational and care programmes to be made compulsory, the paternalistic role of the state is increased and women's freedom to regulate their time and bodily integrity is reduced. The question also arises of how participation might be compelled. One option would be to make the receipt of additional state benefits dependant on attendance at classes and clinics. However, not only is discrimination on the basis of wealth offensive, it would ensure the participation of only a limited number of women. It would be conceivable that courts might order participation and that there might be criminal sanctions, by way of a fine or imprisonment, to support such orders. In the case of educational programmes, this would be unwarranted on the criteria of both necessity and effectiveness. Many women will have access to the relevant information from their own experience, the experience of friends and relatives and from the vast amount of literature available on the subject. Furthermore, the idea of 'compulsory education' is a fallacy, since it amounts to no more than compulsory attendance at a place where it is intended that the education will occur. In the context of antenatal care, involving examination and testing of the pregnant woman, compulsory participation would almost certainly have some benefit in providing early warning of future problems which might then be avoided, but at what price? Since it is impractical to suggest that the state could monitor the entire female population of childbearing age in order to establish who is pregnant at any given time, women who opposed some or all aspects of the care programme would simply not inform the authorities. Where women were indifferent to such care, the fact of their pregnancy would again probably not be known and again, that any compulsory system would be futile. Where the woman's condition was known and she refused to participate in the care programme, despite court order, imprisonment or forced care is both an unacceptable invasion of her freedom and unwarranted, since no specific danger to the fetus could be demonstrated. Furthermore, the presence of such sanctions would discourage women with reservations about aspects of the treatment programme from participating in it at all. It seems, therefore, that educational and health care programmes, while offering great benefits will only be effective through publicity and persuasion.

A second form of intervention would be to prohibit pregnant women from engaging in certain activities and occupations which would otherwise be available to them. To prohibit the consumption of tobacco products and alcohol by pregnant women would be a possible, but wholly unworkable, option. The retailer cannot be expected to know the ultimate consumer of items sold, nor can he or she be expected to know whether or not a particular customer is pregnant. Policing the activities of all pregnant women would be unduly invasive, disproportionately expensive and, in any event, impossible.

In the field of employment, however, it would be possible to provide that any woman who became pregnant should give up a particular job for the duration of her pregnancy. In the UK the relevant legislation permits discrimination against a pregnant woman in the employment context where it can be shown that the purpose of the discrimination is to protect the pregnant woman. While such a prohibition may disrupt the pregnant woman's career, it can be justified, subject to certain conditions. First, there must be clear evidence that continuing in the particular field of employment creates risks to the fetus which are in excess, or substantially in excess, of those encountered in everyday life. Secondly, the woman must either be offered suitable alternative employment or be given full compensation for all financial loss suffered as a result of giving up her job. Thirdly, there should be a presumption that she will be entitled to reinstatement, with no loss of promotion or other benefits, within a specified period after she has given birth. There may be a very small number of cases, involving highly specialized types of work, where it will not be possible for an employer to do this, but the onus must be on the employer to demonstrate that this is the case. In this situation, the woman should be entitled to full compensation for all loss sustained while she finds suitable alternative employment.

Clearly, this would be expensive and, it is submitted, the full cost should be borne by the state. If employers were expected to finance all or part of the scheme, the burden on small businesses would be considerable and would result there, and possibly in larger enterprises, in a reluctance to employ women of childbearing age. Furthermore, if the state, representing its own interests and those of future children, mandates restrictions on the rights of pregnant women, then it should pay the price. To put this in another way, if we as the individuals of which our society is composed claim an interest in the welfare of future children then we should share the burden of achieving that goal.

Where a pregnant woman persists, in the face of all advice and available evidence, in pursuing a course of action which creates a substantial risk of harm to the child which she will bear, the question arises of what, if any, form of intervention might be legitimate. It is unlikely that a court order of a fine would be effective in controlling behaviour, particularly where that behaviour was not wholly voluntary. For instance, an alcoholic or a heroin addict might realize the dangers her addiction was creating and want to stop taking the particular substance, but find that she was unable to do so. The only way to prevent her from continuing to take the substance would be to deny her access to it and the only way to achieve this end would appear to be continuous supervision or detention, always assuming that it is possible to ensure that persons detained are prevented from gaining access to controlled substances. Clearly, this involves a major intrusion on the woman's freedom, perhaps all the more so where her conduct was not itself illegal. The benefit would be in avoiding harm which would otherwise be caused to the child. To weigh these two factors against each other would be a difficult task in itself, but there are further problems. An addict who realized that continuation of her pregnancy would result in a period of detention might well opt for an abortion which she would not have had otherwise. While the present author supports the right of every woman to make her own choice on the question of abortion, it is quite a different matter for her to be pushed into that decision by the legal system. Furthermore, the possibility of detention might deter an addict from seeking any antenatal advice or care at all, thereby losing the opportunity of counselling and help which would otherwise have been available to her. The case against detention in terms of its effectiveness in avoiding harm and the tremendous infringement of women's liberty would, therefore, appear to be a strong one. Nonetheless, the possibility should not be completely dismissed. Where the probability of harm resulting from the woman's conduct is high and all other means of persuasion have failed, this radical solution seems the only way to prevent a child from facing life with a disability that could have been avoided. While this response should be adopted sparingly, if at all, it might be appropriate in some circumstances. If this radical restriction of a woman's freedom is thought to be justified in a particular case, it should be borne in mind that the prospect of detention could have detrimental consequences in the wider context.

Another possible approach to protecting the fetus would be for the court to grant a supervisory or custodial right over it to a third party or to invoke its own wardship jurisdiction. No case on this point has arisen in Scotland, as yet. However, courts in England, the USA and Canada have had the opportunity to consider the question.

In England, a local authority applied to the court to have a fetus, being carried by a woman who was suffering from severe mental disturbance, engaged in periodic drug abuse and lived a nomadic existence, made a ward of court.[39] The court rejected the application on the grounds that it would be an undue restriction on the rights of the woman and that it would create a conflict between her rights and those of the fetus. One might be forgiven for pointing out that the conflict already existed and that the decision avoided addressing the question of where the balance lay.

In the USA, a Social Services Department applied for custody of a fetus being carried by a woman who had previously abused her child.[40] Initially the order was granted, but this was overturned on appeal on the basis that, in the particular statute involved, the word 'child' could not be deemed to include the fetus. It is interesting to note that the appeal court continued the original custody order for sixty days, by which time the baby would be born. This would enable the Social Services Department to exercise custody over and to protect the child from birth, pending a final determination on the matter of custody.

While both of these cases were concerned with the court's jurisdiction over the fetus, the latter was really an attempt to deal with the issue of child protection, since there appears to have been no risk until the child was born. In the English case, however, the question of control of the fetus' environment was at issue, although the court missed the opportunity to explore the interests involved.

In Canada, the courts have addressed the question. In Ontario, custody of a thirty-eight week old fetus was awarded to the Children's Aid Society for three months.[41] There, the pregnant woman was experiencing severe abdominal pain and was living in underground parking garages. It is significant that the court also ordered her to be hospitalized for medical assessment, since it found reasonable cause to believe that she was suffering from a mental disorder. In a subsequent case in British Columbia, a similar decision was reached.[42]

In practice, taking control of the fetus inevitably means controlling the pregnant woman and is subject to the same objections and practical obstacles. Indeed, it achieves, by means of a different legal mechanism, the same result as subjecting the woman to detention during her pregnancy. In this respect, it is a less honest confrontation of the conflicting interests involved.

A further example of intervention, directed at the fetus, but inevitably affecting the woman, is court ordered medical treatment. Where a woman refuses to submit to a form of medical or surgical treatment recommended by her physician as necessary to save the fetus, the question of compelling her to comply with the advice arises. It is generally accepted that a competent adult will not be compelled to undergo treatment, even if, in the absence of such treatment, death will result.[43] However, courts have been willing to override parental objection in authorizing treatment of children, including that which is not necessary to save the child's life.[44] The courts in the UK have not, as yet, had the opportunity to consider the question of compelling a pregnant woman to undergo treatment, but the issue has been litigated in the USA.

As early as 1964, a court in New Jersey authorized hospital personnel to administer a blood transfusion to a pregnant woman who objected to such treatment on religious grounds, should it prove necessary to save the thirty-two week old fetus.[45] More recently, controversy has surrounded the issue of 'forced caesarians'.[46] In *Jefferson v Griffin Spalding County Hospital Authority*,[47] the hospital petitioned the court for authority to perform a caesarian section and any necessary blood transfusion on Jefferson should she enter the hospital. She had previously made clear that she had a religious objection to such a course of action. Evidence was lead to the effect that there was a ninety-nine per cent chance that the child would not survive vaginal delivery. The court granted the order requested and the Supreme Court of Georgia refused to overturn that decision. Ironically, Jefferson was delivered of a healthy baby without surgical intervention a few days later. Caesarian delivery was ordered by a Colorado court in a subsequent case.[48]

Clearly, these decisions infringe both the woman's bodily integrity and freedom of religion. The courts in the cases above felt this was justified in order to save the baby. The courts have not been 'willing to order treatment unless it was satisfied that it was necessary'.[49] Nor, it is submitted, would it authorize treatment if the result would be to sacrifice the life of the woman in order to save the child. In this context, the subordination of a woman's rights appears justified.

One further issue arises in this context – that of performing a caesarian section on a pregnant woman in the final stages of terminal illness, where the operation might hasten her death. In principle, shortening the life of a human being presents the same problems whether the period of time involved is twenty-four hours or twenty-four years. In practice, the balancing of interests becomes more difficult where the possibility of shortening the pregnant woman's life by a very short time involves the possibility of saving that of the child. This was one of the dilemmas confronted by the court in Re A.C.[50] There, a terminally ill patient was in her twenty-sixth week of pregnancy. She had discussed the possibility of a caesarian delivery at twenty-eight weeks, but at the time of the petition, she was heavily sedated and unable to express an opinion. It was acknowledged that the surgery might hasten her death by between twenty-four and forty-eight hours, but that this would give the baby some chance of survival. Her death prior to the performance of a caesarian section would have resulted in the death of the baby as well. The operation was ordered by the court and sadly neither the woman nor the child survived. Did the court do the right thing? At least it tried to save a life albeit at the cost of shortening another.

The forms of intervention discussed above all aim at preventing harm before it occurs. The next two forms of intervention might be described as preventing harm only in so far as they deter pregnant women from particular behaviour. Holding the mother liable in damages for antenatal injury sustained by the child involves the idea of compensation while criminal sanctions add the dimension of punishment.

Third party liability for antenatal injury is now well established. The Scottish Law Commission had no difficulty in accepting, in 1974, that the principles of delictual liability applied equally to the child's mother and felt that any change in the law would require further consideration and public consultation.[51] While the courts have not had the opportunity to consider the matter, there have been no attempts to alter the law and no voices raised in support of such a move. In England and Wales, the Law Commission there initially supported maternal liability for antenatal injury.[52] However, after consultation, it rejected that view in favour of confining liability to situations where the mother was driving a motor vehicle.[53] The latter preference found expression in the current legislation.[54]

In the USA, opinion is divided. In *Grodin v Grodin*,[55] it was alleged that a woman did not inform her physician that she might be pregnant and took tetracycline prescribed for her. At a later date, she sought further medical advice and, on discovering that she was seven or eight months pregnant, stopped taking the medication. As a result of her taking the drug during pregnancy, her son developed brown, discoloured teeth. His action for damages for injury sustained as a result of her negligence in failing to alert her physician to the possibility of pregnancy was held admissable. In *Stallman v Youngquist*,[56] it was alleged that the injury sustained by the child resulted from a car accident caused, at least in part, by her mother's negligent driving. The court rejected her claim on the basis that to allow it would impose an undue burden on pregnant women and that, for liability to exist, the court would have to define an acceptable standard of behaviour for pregnant women – a task which it felt unable to undertake. Furthermore, while the court accepted that the fiction by which a fetus was viewed as nothing other than a part of the pregnant woman had been correctly rejected in the context of third party liability, to suggest that the two were entirely separate entities was to create a fiction of another sort. It is interesting to note that the court rejected liability in the only situation where the English courts would have permitted recovery.

It is submitted that both the English legislation and the court in *Stallman* give undue weight to the rights of pregnant women in balancing them against the right of the injured child to compensation. All members of society have restrictions placed upon their conduct where that conduct might cause injury to others. The restrictions faced by pregnant women may be more invasive than those placed on others, but the harm which could result from failure to observe these restrictions may be considerable. In any event, the restrictions are temporary and of a fairly short duration. Where the woman fails to observe the restrictions and injury results, it appears entirely reasonable that the victim should be compensated. It is acknowledged that, in some cases, the mother will not be in a position to pay the damages awarded. However, that is not a reason to deny compensation to those who can recover. Where there is no prospect of recovery from the mother, it is unlikely that actions would be raised but, even here, compensation could be provided by a state scheme.

There remains the question of whether or not criminal liability should attach to the mother's antenatal conduct. There is little case law in this area. In *Reyes v Superior Court*,[57] a woman who had continued to take heroin throughout her pregnancy, despite warnings as to the possible consequences, gave birth to twins suffering from heroin addiction and, subsequently, withdrawal symptoms. She was charged with felonious child endangering, but the charge was dismissed on the ground that the statute was not intended to cover the antenatal situation.

The case of *Pamela Rae Stewart*[58] was dismissed before it reached trial and a number of the facts are disputed and unproven, but the fact that she was charged with an offence is, in itself, significant. At the end of her ninth month of pregnancy she gave birth to a brain dead son. He was placed in intensive care, released into foster care five weeks later and died after a few days. It was alleged that she had failed to follow medical advice during her pregnancy regarding her conduct, the taking of medication and seeking immediate assistance if bleeding occurred. It was also alleged that she took amphetamines and marijuana during pregnancy, an allegation supported by the results of toxicology screenings of herself and the baby directly after the birth. She was charged under a California statute dealing with failure to provide a child with necessary care, this charge being dismissed later. Her background was unsettled. She lived with her husband and two daughters in various motels and trailer homes, relying on the husband's itinerant jobs for the family income. He had been violent towards her, the children had been placed in care and there was a strong association with drug abuse. It is in this sort of socio-economic setting that the question of prosecution might often arise.

It is doubtful that the prospect of prosecution would have any deterrent effect in such cases. Thus, any prevention of injury to the fetus would be negligible. The only effect of prosecution would be to express social disapproval of the woman's conduct and to punish her for it. This implies that her conduct was voluntary, a proposition which is hard to defend where economic circumstances or addiction play a prominent role. Were criminal liability to be accepted as a valid response, it is imperative that background circumstances should play a part in sentencing decisions.

It had been argued above that, in order to avoid injury to the fetus, certain restriction may validly be placed on the freedom of action of the pregnant woman. In order to be justified the restriction in question must not only be effective in avoiding a proven harm, it must be capable of practical application not offset by disproportionate intrusion in the lives of the individuals involved. Furthermore, where society takes it upon itself to regulate the antenatal environment, it must be prepared to pay the price by providing adequate antenatal care and counselling, financial support and housing for the women who are to meet the standards set.

(I would like to thank the Carnegie Trust for the Universities in Scotland for its generous support which enabled me to pursue much of the research upon which this chapter is based.)

Notes

1. *Walker v Great Northern Railway Co. of Ireland* (1891) 28 Ir.L.R. 69; *Dietrich v Inhabitants of Northampton* 138 Mass. 14 (1884).
2. *Montreal Tramways v Leveille* (1933) 4 Dom.L.R. 337.
3. Report on Liability for Antenatal Injury, Scot. Law Com. No. 30, 1973, para. 19.
4. Winfield and Jolowicz, Torts, 9th ed., Butterworth, London 1971, at p. 116; Street, Torts, 5th ed. Butterworths, London, 1972, at p. 109n.
5. Report on Injuries to Unborn Children, Law Com. No. 60, 1974, paras. 3 and 8.
6. Section 1. It should be noted that the Act specifically excludes the mother's liability, except where the injury occurs as a result of her driving a motor vehicle.
7. *Dietrich, supra: Allaire v St. Luke's Hospital* 184 Ill. 359 (1900); *Drobner v Peters* 232 N.Y. 220 (1921); *Magnolia Coca Cola Bottling Co v. Jordan* 124 Tex. 347 (1935).
8. See, for example, *Bonbrest v Kotz* 65 Fed. Supp. 138 (1946); *Smith v Brennan* 157 A. 2d 497 (1960, N.J.) where Proctor J. provided an excellent review of the development of the principle of recovery for antenatal injury in the USA.
9. *Hollis v Commonwealth of Kentucky* 652 S.W. 2d 61 (1983, Ky.).

10. *McCluskey v H.M.A.* 1989 S.L.T. 175.
11. *Commonwealth v Cass* 467 N.E. 2d 1324 (1984, Mass.).
12. *R. v Tait* [1989] 3 All ER. 682.
13. Where the carrier is a surrogate, the participation of the 'commissioning parents' in decision making raises interesting questions which are unfortunately outwith the scope of this discussion.
14. *Re F* 351 N.Y.S. 2d 337 (1974); *Baby X* 293 N.W. 2d 736 (1980, Mich.); *Re D (a minor) v Berkshire County Council* [1987] 1 All ER. 20.
15. For an excellent discussion of the effects of the most commonly used drugs, see, Larson, *Intoxication in Utero*, in Mason (ed.), *Paediatric Forensic Medicine and Pathology*, Chapman and Hall, London, 1989.
16. See, for example, *S. v Distillers and Co. (Biochemicals) Ltd.* [1970] 1W.L.R. 114, where the Thalidomide tragedy is discussed.
17. Article 12, which acknowledges the right to marry and to found a family.
18. *Gleitman v Cosgrove* 227 A. 2d 689 (1967, N.J.).
19. *Speck v Finnegold* 408 A. 2d 496 (1979, Pa.).
20. *Berman v Allan* 404 A. 2d 8 (1979, N.J.).
21. *Gildener v Thomas Jefferson University Hospital* 451 F. Supp. 692 (1978, Pa.).
22. 106 Cal. App. 3d 811 (1980).
23. *Turpin v Sortini* 643 P. 2d 954 (1982, Cal.); *Harbeson v Parke-Davis* 659 P. 2d 483 (1983, Wash.); *Gallacher v Duke University* 638 F. Supp. 979 (1988, N.C.).
24. *Thake v Maurice* [1984] 2 All ER. 513; *Emeh v Kensington Area Health Authority* [1984] 3 All ER. 1044; cf. *Udale v Bloomsbury Area Health Authority* [1983] 2 All ER. 522. In *Gold v Haringey Area Health Authority* [1987] 2 All ER. 888, the claim was refused on the ground that sufficient warning of the possible ineffectiveness of the operation had been given.
25. *McKay v Essex Area Health Authority* [1982] 2 All ER. 711.
26. Note 22, *supra*, at p. 829.
27. In *Cleveland Board of Education v LaFleur* 414 U.S. 416 (1983), the Supreme Court held unconstitutional a rule requiring every pregnant schoolteacher to take five months unpaid leave prior to the birth of her child.
28. Note 17, *supra*.
29. See Jonsen, 'The Creation of Fetal Rights: Conflicts with Women's Constitutional Rights to Liberty, Privacy and Equal Protection', 95 Yale L.J. 599 (1986), at pp. 605–609.
30. *Roe v Wade* 410 U.S. 113 (1973).
31. Abortion Act 1967.
32. See p. 100, *supra*.
33. See p. 101, *supra*.
34. See p. 101, *supra*.

35. In Scotland, for example, see *Elliot v Joicey* 1935 S.C. (H.L.) 57.
36. In Scotland, for example, see *Leadbetter v N.C.B.* 1952 S.L.T. 179.
37. See pp. 114–116.
38. The Employment Act 1989, s. 3, amending the Sex Discrimination Act 1975, s. 51. For a discussion of some of the problems associated with such an approach see Thowsend-Smith, *Sex Discrimination: Law and Practice* (1989), pp. 130–133; Conoghan and Cudleigh, 'Women in Confinement: can labour law deliver the goods?' (1987) 14 J. Law and Soc. 133; Finley, 'Transcending Equality Theory: a way out of the maternity and workplace debate', 86 Col. L. Rev. 118 (1986).
39. *Re F (in utero)* [1988] 2 All ER. 193.
40. *Bay County of Social Services, in re Dittrick*, Infant 263 N.W. 2d 37 (1977, Mich.).
41. *Children's Aid Society and Unborn Child of L.T. and G.K.*, noted in The Guardian, National Association of Counsel for Children, U.S.A., Vol. 9, Summer 1987, p. 7.
42. Noted in The Guardian, National Association of Counsel for Children, USA, Vol. 9, Fall 1987, p. 6.
43. *Whitehall v Whitehall* 1958 S.C. 252; *In re Conroy* 486 A. 2d 1209 (1985, N.J.); *John F. Kennedy Memorial Hospital v Bludworth* 452 So. 2d 291 (1984, Fla.).
44. *Finlayson* 1989 S.C.L.R. 601; *In re Philip B.* 92 Cal. App. 3d 796 (1979); *In re Cicero* 101 Misc. 2d 699 (1979, N.Y.).
45. *Raleigh Fitkin-Paul Memorial Hospital v Anderson* 201 A. 2d 537 (1964, N.J.), cert. denied, 377 U.S. 985 (1964).
46. Annas, 'Forced Cesarians: The Most Unkindest Cut Of All', 12 Hastings Center Report, 16 (1982); Rhoden, 'The Judge in the Delivery Room: The Emergence of Court-Ordered Cesarians', 74 Cal. L. Rev. 1951 (1986).
47. 274 S.E. 2d 457 (1981, Ga.).
48. This case is discussed in Annas, note 46, *supra*. See also, *In re Maydun*, D.C. Super. Ct. July 26, 1986, unrep., where a caesarian section was ordered in the face of maternal opposition.
49. *Taft v Taft* 446 N.E. 2d 395 (1983, Mass.).
50. 539 A. 2d 203 (1988, D.C.).
51. Note 3, *supra*.
52. Injuries to Unborn Children, Working Paper No. 47, 1973, para. 27.
53. Report on Injuries to Unborn Children, Law Com. No. 60, 1974, para. 63.
54. Congenital Disabilities (Civil Liability) Act 1976, ss. 1(1) and 2.
55. 101 Mich. App. 396 (1980).
56. 531 N.E. 2d 355 (1988, Ill.).
57. 75 Cal. App. 2d 214 (1977).
58. Johnsen, 'A New Threat to Pregnant Women's Autonomy', 17 Hastings Center Reports (1987) at p. 33.

7. Mothers and others: the case for surrogacy
Sheila A. M. McLean

'The body of a woman should not be for sale or rent'
Under the headline 'Panelist Denounces Surrogate Motherhood' *National*, in September 1988, reported Jean Louis Baudouin, an editor of the Canadian Bar Review, as having commented on surrogacy in the terms quoted above. His comments highlight some of the concern which surrounds this most contentious aspect of modern reproductive technology. It is perhaps not overstating the case to say that of all of the modern reproductive techniques, it is surrogacy which has generated a large part of the anxiety that medicine and science are outstripping public morality. Roberts notes that 'surrogate motherhood poses a difficult challenge for society and the law.'[1]

Opinions on the rightness or wrongness of surrogacy have stultified legal development, and – some might say – have caused such controversy that other (and apparently less contentious) new reproductive techniques have been largely ignored by the law. This is true to the extent that (until now) the only legislation directly relating to modern reproductive techniques in the United Kingdom has been the Surrogacy Arrangements Act 1985, outlawing commercial surrogacy arrangements.[2]

It is, of course, the case that virtually all novel reproductive techniques have generated interest and concern. Techniques such as artificial insemination, now regarded as relatively standard medical treatment, have in their day caused considerable problems. Despite their general acceptance by the law and by society, they have been the subject of legal argument in the past and were denounced as illegal and immoral.[3]

The speed with which reproductive technology has progressed has left society and the law gasping for breath. New and complex moral and legal dilemmas emerge with every advance, and no answers to these problems seem obvious. Since the publication of the Warnock Report in 1984[4] legislation has been promised for the United Kingdom – a promise which seemed likely to be met in the Parliamentary Session 1989–90.[5]

Of all of the available options, however, few have generated such heated debate as has the potential for medically controlled surrogacy. As Cusine,[6] amongst others, has pointed out, natural surrogacy is scarcely a new phenomenon. It has always been pragmatically possible for women to conceive a child with the intention of handing that child over after its birth, and doubtless this has happened on a number of (unregistered and unnoticed) occasions. Indeed, as long ago as 1978 British Courts were faced with resolving just such a dilemma in the case of *A. v. C.*[7] What distinguishes modern day surrogacy, however, is the potential to use women as surrogates on a larger and more controlled scale. If anything, this has generated an increased moral outcry, although arguably surrogacy which does not involve adultery (as its older version would have done) might seem to be less objectionable than its previous form.

Be that as it may, the controversy surrounding surrogate arrangements remains acute. Before considering the arguments for and against surrogacy, it is worth describing exactly what it is. Fundamentally, surrogacy could take three distinct forms, but in all of them the ultimate intention is that the gestational 'mother' intends to hand the child over at birth to the commissioning couple who intend to raise the child in their family. It is appropriate to use the word 'couple' because no jurisdiction (to my knowledge) will countenance the provision of a surrogate arrangement to a single commissioning person.[8]

In the first case, it could involve a woman, carrying to term a fetus whose genetic material is provided by donors who are not the commissioning couple. In this case, none of the participants, apart from the egg and sperm donors, would have any biological relationship to the subsequent child. In the second case, a woman may carry to term a fetus whose biological parents are the commissioning couple; and in the third case (partial surrogacy) the carrying mother may have been inseminated with the sperm of the male partner of the commissioning couple.

The first two of these options arguably represent no more than an extension of artificial insemination, and the third is a clear example of it. Nonetheless, whilst artificial insemination seems to attract few moral objections nowadays, it remains the case that surrogacy is perceived as being different and infinitely more problematic. The woman who donates the use of her womb is seen as being, in a fundamentally important way, different from the man who donates his semen. Undoubtedly there are at least practical differences between carrying a fetus throughout the normal gestation period and the donation of ejaculate, but the question remains whether or not these differences are truly of a moral nature, or whether they merely are used as a vehicle for expressing distaste or reinforcing gender stereotypes.

Although the arguments for and against surrogacy have been widely rehearsed[9] it is worthwhile briefly to restate the major ones. In so doing, it is also essential to bear in mind that – although surrogacy simpliciter is often confused with paid surrogacy – the concept of surrogacy itself need not include the transfer of any financial rewards or inducements. Those who oppose surrogacy sometimes seem to introduce the financial element as a method of demonstrating what is wrong with it, and certainly some of their arguments directly attack only paid surrogacy. But these arguments contain different and distinct elements which can reasonably be dealt with separately. Further, as Freeman[10] points out, the Warnock Report was somewhat disingenuous in its consideration of this subject, dealing first with what they called surrogacy 'for convenience'. This last is surely the most contentious aspect of surrogacy and might better have been considered after careful analysis of surrogacy in general rather than before it.

In order to review the arguments for and against surrogacy, therefore, a distinction will be made between those arguments which concern surrogacy *per se*, and those which affect only paid surrogacy. In addition, it must be said that some of the arguments concern the woman who is infertile and some concern the would-be surrogate herself. Again, it is common to elide these and to ignore the fact that there are subtle reasons for differentiating them – reasons which may change the tone of the debate. Account will also be taken of those arguments which concern the child. Depending on our conclusions about these, surrogate arrangements which do not involve an infertile woman will be considered.

The arguments for surrogacy

Briefly, these can be summarized under the following headings:

A – *Arguments relating to the infertile*

1) It seems to be accepted generally that the circumvention of infertility is a good thing. Yet, for some couples such circumvention is impossible unless surrogacy is permitted. For the woman whose uterus is removed as a result of a cancerous condition, but who continues to ovulate, for example, no biological link with a child is

feasible unless it is possible to find another woman prepared to carry an embryo on her behalf. The only option, therefore, is adoption – notoriously difficult, and also an option available to all other childless couples. The question which must be posed therefore is why certain *causes* of infertility should not be circumvented when the outcome of different techniques (that is, the creation and birth of a wanted child) is the same whatever the method used?

2) Some women may find it unwise to carry a child, for example on the basis of a serious risk to their general health associated with pregnancy. Or it may be that a particular woman runs considerable risk of passing on a congenital problem to a child and would therefore be advised to avoid conception. Partial surrogacy would answer this problem and result in a child which is at least genetically related to her partner. Are these women to be denied the possibility of parenting?

B – Arguments relating to potential surrogates

3) A woman, it might be argued, has a right to do with her body as she chooses. A woman may, therefore, choose to act as a surrogate mother because she is the person directly affected by this choice, and so long as it does not cause harm to others, she is entitled to make this decision in the same way as she might make other choices which may entail some risk to herself but which are essentially within the scope of her right to self-determination.

C – Arguments relating to the child

4) It must always be better to be alive than never to have had the chance to be born. Outlawing surrogacy denies existence to a potential child. The preference for life over death is one which has featured in exactly this form in arguments concerning wrongful life actions in this country and elsewhere. Courts have generally endorsed the view that the gift of a child is always a joy, and that it is irrational to argue that it would be better never to have been born at all.[11]

5) The child who is conceived in this way will likely be a very much wanted child, and likely therefore to have a happy life.

Arguments against surrogacy

A – Arguments which relate to the infertile

1) It is always wrong to use another as a means to an end. Thus, the infertile woman has no right to seek another woman to carry a child

for her, since by so doing she threatens the inherent value of the other woman whom she is using in this way.

B — *Arguments which relate to the potential surrogate*

2) Surrogacy exploits women. Women, it may be said, are, whilst apparently making a free choice, actually being coerced into agreeing to act as a surrogate by some subliminal pressure. Thus, a sister may feel obliged to carry a child for her infertile sibling, or a woman with many children may feel moral pressure to help other (infertile) women by bearing a child for them. It should be noted that at this point it is also usual to introduce evidence about paid surrogacy, but this writer will not do this. Altruistic surrogacy can and should be distinguished at this stage. Effectively, therefore, this argument says that women who make an apparently altruistic choice are in fact pressurized into it and should be protected from this if they are not to be in danger of being exploited. One is forced to ask, however, whether *any* apparently altruistic choice is actually that straightforward. Moreover, one must also question whether it is the function of the law to prevent people from making altruistic choices – even self-interested choices – unless real harm to others can be shown.

3) Women should not deliberately conceive with the intention of giving up the subsequent child. To permit this, or to facilitate it, threatens our view of society as a whole and motherhood in particular.

C — *Arguments relating to the child*

4) The child born as the result of such an arrangement may never know his or her true parents. They will be genetically anomic. As a result of this, they may suffer psychologically. The argument concerning children has been described as 'the most substantial argument against surrogacy'[12] and certainly, were such damage a real risk then this would represent a powerful reason not to permit surrogate arrangements.

5) If something goes wrong then the child may also suffer. For example, if the commissioning parents don't accept the child, if the surrogate also won't keep it, or the surrogate refuses to hand it over, then there is potential harm to the child.[13]

The above, admittedly extremely brief, outline of the arguments used by those who are for or against surrogacy highlight some interesting characteristics of the debate. There are, of course, additional arguments but these will be left aside for the moment since they concern paid and/or commercial surrogacy and not surrogacy in itself.

What is particularly interesting is that the first two sections in each argument are women-centred. In the arguments for surrogacy, the infertile woman features strongly in a somewhat passive, but intelligible, role. In the arguments against surrogacy, the woman again is focused upon, although this time the assumption is that she needs to be protected from herself. But what both have in common is the underlying assumptions about women themselves. The woman who desperately desires a child and for whom surrogacy is the only, or the preferred, option, is regarded with sympathy. It is after all entirely intelligible that women will want to have children. But it is apparently unintelligible that a woman might wish to have a child for someone else. Indeed, it is tempting to suggest that it is this threat to what society regards as the 'normal' way for a woman to behave that really underlies many of the arguments against surrogacy. The juxtaposing of a woman who desperately wants a child and a woman who is prepared to give one away throws our basic presuppositions about the role of women into stark relief.

However, I have already conceded that if the arguments in respect of children are strong enough then they might well be determinative of the view we should take of surrogacy. It is, presumably, unarguable that the arguments which form part of the pro-surrogacy point of view are sound. They therefore require little further discussion. Giving life is not likely to be regarded as a bad thing. But the arguments used in the anti-surrogacy point of view also carry some weight.

The first argument, that the child may suffer psychologically from not being informed about his or her genetic background is, however, at best speculative, and it certainly is not irrevocably true. As Roberts[14] points out, many children already do live in families where they are being raised by adults who did not conceive them and we have little, if any, reason to assume that they are fundamentally unhappy or in some way psychologically disturbed. Indeed, if this were the case, then we should have to rethink our attitude to adoption. What will be likely to cause harm, however, is being a child of a surrogate arrangement in a society which is – however illogically – opposed to such arrangements, and makes its opposition known. Given the relatively prevalent temptation to despise or abuse those who are different, this represents a real fear. It is, however, also in our hands to change it, by adopting a more rational approach to surrogacy itself, or by authorizing the commissioning couple to declare themselves parents for the purpose of birth registration, thereby avoiding the problems altogether.

The second argument concerns potential harm when the arrangement itself breaks down. Undoubtedly, as the case of *Baby* M[15] has shown, the spectacle of people fighting over a baby is unedifying, and the potential for harm to the child throughout its life is certainly there. But what is particularly unedifying about it is the fact that it could be avoided. Careful and thoughtful regulation of surrogacy arrangements can avoid many of the difficulties which might arise in a 'tug-of-love' situation like this, and the child who is rejected by both surrogate and commissioning couple on the grounds of handicap is no worse off than those who are rejected on the same grounds by their natural parents. In any event, it is not playing entirely straight to argue from what would probably be a tiny minority of cases to reach the conclusion that the majority is wrong.

Given, therefore, that it is accepted that the arguments from the child and against surrogacy are not insurmountable, we are left with the possibility of reassessing the arguments concerning the participants. I would argue that the arguments against surrogacy which concentrate on the potential surrogate hold no water. Few of us ever do an entirely altruistic act and even fewer of us would relish being 'protected' by the apparatus of the state from the consequences of our own choices, particularly when we believe ourselves to be doing good and when there is no obvious victim of our behaviour – indeed, there are only obvious winners.

It can be concluded, therefore, that there is nothing inherent in surrogacy itself which would justify invasion of the liberty of citizens to enter into such an arrangement. But does this conclusion change if money or other inducement is involved? In other words, is the practice one which can only be supported if done without recompense?

Surrogacy for reward

It is clear that it is the possibility of the introduction of a financial element into surrogacy arrangements which generates the majority of criticism. Even those who do not oppose surrogacy in principle, often reject the morality of introducing financial considerations into the creation and rearing of a child. Paid surrogacy is, it is said, equivalent to 'baby selling' and therefore strikes against the respect due to human beings. Pointing to the prohibition in the adoption legislation on the transfer of money, it is widely agreed that the same restrictions should be applied in cases of surrogacy. Yet at least one British court has refused to declare adoption proceedings unlawful even though the child to be adopted was the result of a surrogacy agreement in which payment was made.[16] Of course, this was a *post facto* decision, and doesn't affect the argument that such agreements should not be entered into, since the court – when confronted with the situation – has the responsibility of having direct concern for the best interests of the (now existing) child.

There are, however, two distinct situations in which money may be involved in surrogacy, and arguably they raise different problems, and may, indeed, lead to different conclusions. The first is where the surrogate mother is paid for the service of conceiving and carrying a child. Proponents of payment would argue that the woman should be paid for the service she undoubtedly performs, whilst opponents would claim that the payment is for the child, and therefore that this is merely an aspect of baby selling, and therefore immoral. In addition, it may be said, financial inducements may result in the exploitation of poor women for whom surrogacy represents a real opportunity of improving their lot. Certainly, one surrogate mother, Kim Cotton honestly admitted that money was a major reason for her participation,[17] but research also shows altruistic as well as financial considerations to have played a significant part in the decision of women to become surrogates.[18]

In any event, it might be argued that we are all providing services for money, and that if poor women can improve their situation by this means, then they are in no different a situation from others who engage in employment. The Ontario Law Reform Commission seems to have reached a method of resolving some of the difficulties inherent in paid surrogacy by proposing a detailed regulatory structure, including the requirement that the court should be required to authorize any payment for surrogacy in advance.[19] In the meantime, the Council of Europe, whilst conceding that states may legislate to permit surrogacy, nonetheless expressly indicates that 'the surrogate mother [should obtain] . . . no material benefit from the operation'.[20]

The second situation relates to commercial surrogacy – already outlawed in the United Kingdom. This raises the additional spectre of profiteering from infertility and is generally frowned upon. On the other hand, if the principle is accepted that surrogacy is not *in se* wrong, and if women can be paid for their services, it is not clear that commercial ventures are inherently wrong. This is particularly true where the service is not regularly available elsewhere, and yet represents the only opportunity for a couple to have a child. In addition, where the agency is closely regulated and professionally of optimal standards, it may well serve to fill a gap in the provision of infertility services.

In fact, in many ways, the main problem which I see in surrogacy for payment is that it would restrict the availability of the service to those who have the financial status to benefit from it. In addition, if surrogacy is routinely rewarded it seems likely that *no one* would be prepared to undertake it without payment. Yet there is no doubt that women who act as surrogates *do* perform a valuable service. If this is recognized then should we not permit *some* payment in *all* surrogacy arrangements, but closely regulate the sums which can change hands – perhaps by the establishment of a fixed fee? This would also help to obviate the problems which might arise if surrogates ever do attempt to demand more money. In any event, it seems likely that, since surrogacy will continue with or without medical intervention and with or without social acceptance, the optimum response is to solve (in as far as this is possible) the difficulties surrounding voluntary surrogacy (or surrogacy for a fixed and reasonable fee). In this way, there would be no market for the potential exploitation of commercialization. The esoteric arguments about whether or not payment equals baby selling can be resolved by an act of will – we can choose to agree that payment represents a payment for the service rendered – an approach which is at least as plausible as the other alternative.

The noted reluctance to concede the value of surrogacy arrangements seems, therefore, to reflect an attitude about women's reproductive capacities and conduct, rather than generally mirroring a sense of immorality in the abstract. That this is at the root of the Warnock Committee's attitude[21] seems to be reinforced by their consideration of surrogacy 'for convenience', before they considered other reasons for seeking to enter into such an arrangement. In focusing on this issue, they express their abhorrence of women who *can* reproduce but choose to have children without pregnancy.

The thought that women might seek to take advantage of such a service is apparently almost inexpressibly dreadful. But why should this be the approach adopted, and perhaps even more importantly, on what grounds should the law seek to intervene? Is the law the protector of public morals? Should the law interfere with the free choice of a woman who, for personally valid reasons, chooses not to be pregnant, but wishes to have a child?

The answer to these questions can only be reached if we examine the basis of the general distaste for surrogacy itself. Were it the case that concern was generated by arguments about the welfare of the child, then this might be a strong argument against surrogacy, but it certainly would not permit differentiation of the fertile and the infertile. However, if the distaste for surrogacy relates to entrenched attitudes about gender roles or to notions about bonding and motherhood, then the woman who chooses surrogacy 'for convenience' would evidently offend these sensibilities more than would the woman who is infertile.

The fact that Warnock chose to concentrate the attack on the former in the first instance, confirms the view that our objections to surrogacy are not esoteric and morally unassailable. Rather, they are based on the desire to reinforce traditional patterns and attitudes to women and women's role in the reproductive process. If this is the case, there are a number of conclusions which can be reached.

First; given that surrogate arrangements will continue, regulation is a preferable option to outlawing. Second; the law should adopt a permissive rather than an interventionist approach to the freely made choices of individual women. And finally, that we should address ourselves to the *real* problems of surrogacy, such as the status of the agreement, the status of the child, access arrangements, adoption procedures and so on, rather than obfuscating the issue with preconceived, and potentially discriminatory, attitudes towards women.

Notes

1. Roberts, 'Warnock and Surrogate Motherhood: Sentiment or Argument', in Byrne (ed), *Rights and Wrongs in Medicine*, London: Oxford University Press, 1986, p. 111.
2. Amendments to this legislation are proposed in the Human Fertilisation and Embryology Bill, currently before Parliament. For discussion of the 1985 Act, see Freeman, Commentary on the Surrogacy Arrangements Act 1985, in *Current Law Statutes Annotated*, London: Sweet & Maxwell, 1986.
3. For discussion of the history of reproductive techniques and the current situation, see Cusine, *New Reproductive Techniques*, Aldershot: Gower, 1989.
4. London: HMSO, Cmnd. 9314/1984.
5. Human Fertilisation and Embryology Bill, note 2, *supra*

6. Note 3, *supra*.
7. 8 *Fam. Law* (1978), 170.
8. For consideration of the response of a number of jurisdictions, see McLean (ed), *Law Reform and Human Reproduction*, Aldershot, Dartmouth (in press).
9. cf. Roberts, *loc. cit.*; Freeman, 'Is Surrogacy Exploitative?' in McLean (ed), *Legal Issues in Human Reproduction*, Aldershot: Gower, 1989; Morgan, 'Surrogacy: An Introductory Essay' in Lee, and Morgan (eds), *Birthrights: Law and Ethics at the Beginning of Life*, London: Routledge, 1989.
10. Freeman, note 2, *supra*.
11. cf. *McKay v. Essex Area Health Authority* [1982] 2 W.L.R. 890.
12. Freeman, note 2, *supra*, p. 175.
13. The question of harm to the child was considered very seriously by the British Medical Association in the guidelines issued to doctors in respect of surrogacy and reported in *300 British Medical Journal*, 17 March 1990, pp. 752–3. The BMA point to 15 risks which they regard as 'peculiar to a surrogate pregnancy' (p. 753) including a number which specifically relate to children.
14. Note 1, *supra*.
15. 525 A 2d 1128 (1987, NJ).
16. *Adoption Application 212/86* 'The Times' 12 March 1986.
17. See Cotton and Winn, *Baby Cotton: For Love and Money*, London: Dorling Kindersley, 1985.
18. cf. Parker, 'Motivation of Surrogate Mothers: Initial Findings' *140 American Journal of Psychiatry* (1983), 117.
19. Recommendation 51. For a full discussion see Dickens, 'The Ontario Law Reform Commission's Project on Human Artificial Reproduction' in McLean (ed), *Law reform and Human Reproduction*, note 8, *supra*.
20. 'Human Artificial Procreation', Report by the Committee of experts on progress in the biomedical sciences (CAHBI), Strasbourg, 1989, Principle 15 (4) (a).
21. Note 4, *supra*.

Index

Abortion
   following prenatal testing, 54
   in multiple pregnancy, 32
   and minors, 15, 59
   on genetic grounds, 45
   woman's right to, 4, 105, 111
Adoption, 38, 88
AIDS (and HIV), 30, 70, 101
Amniocentesis, 43
Ante-natal injury, 100 et seq
Anti-progesterones, 83
Artificial insemination, 26, 44, 47
Autonomy, 4-6

Best interests test, 67-9, 76

Caesarian section, 114
Child
   contraception and, 13, 84 et seq.
   handicapped, 5, 11
   medical treatment, 11, 16, 17, 59, 70 et seq.
   right to decide on abortion, 15, 59
   right to genetic information, 57
   sexual abuse, 17, 18
Chorion biopsy, 43
Confidentiality in genetic testing, 56
Consent
   of minor to medical treatment, 84 et seq.
   of parent to medical treatment of child, 11, 59 et seq.
Contraception, 13, 14, 80 et seq.
Contragestion, 81
Criminal liability for fetal abuse, 116
Cryopreservation, 33, 34, 38
Custody, 28

Declaration of Helsinki, 62

Donation, 26, 27, 29
Down's Syndrome, 11, 71

Edwards, Dr Robert, 27
Embryos, frozen, ownership of, 33-6
European Convention on Human Rights, 104

Family
   general concept of, 21
   history of, 22
   the new family, 21
   role of, in medical treatment decisions, 59 et seq.
   single parent, 22
Feminism, 23
Fertilisation, in vitro, 27, 32-6
Fetus
   damage to, 100 et seq.
   custody of, 112

Gamete transfer, 26, 28-31
Genetic counselling
   access to, 44
   effect of counselling on decision to have children, 46
   circumstances leading to requests for counselling, 46
Genetic diseases, 42
Genetic engineering, 43
Genetic fingerprinting, 31
Genetic information, ownership of, 45, 53
Genetic testing, control of, 55-7
GIFT, 27
Grief and bereavement, 48

Human Fertilisation and Embryology Bill (UK), 36

Index

Huntingdon's disease
  incidence of, 48
  effect of, 49
  genetic transmissibility of, 49
  psychological impact on sufferer and family, 50
  tests for, 51

Illegitimacy, 21
Incest, 31, 39
Incompetent patient, 64, 69
Informed consent doctrine, 62, 72
Infanticide, 5
Infertility, 23-6
  governmental and religious attitudes towards, 25
  surrogacy and, 122, 123
Intra-uterine device, 82
Inheritance, 21, 30, 44

Kuhse, Helga, 5

Legal liability of doctors, 62
'Life and death' decisions, 59 et seq.

Mason, J. K., 71
Mater est quam gestatio demonstrat, 30, 36
Medical treatment
  court-ordered, 74-5, 113
  family role in, 59 et seq.
  withdrawal of, 70
Menstrual extraction, 83
Mentally-handicapped, sterilisation of, 91 et seq.
Minor (see 'child')
Miscarriage, 82
Maternal behaviour towards fetus, 101 et seq.

Newborn child, 70 et seq.

Parens patriae jurisdiction, 73
Parental immunity, 29
Parental rights, 6 et seq., 73, 86 et seq., 96
Paternalism, 61
Paternity, 30
Patria potestas, 8, 59
Post-coital pill, 83
Power of attorney legislation, 69
Pregnancy
  behaviour during, 102 et seq.
  court-ordered medical treatment during, 113
  rights during, 110
  selective reduction of, 32
Prenatal diagnosis, 42
Proxy decision-making, 65 et seq.

Recombinant DNA technology, 43
Right to die, 60
Rights, parental (see 'parental')
Roman Catholic Church, 15, 25
RU 486, 83

Scottish Law Commission, 89, 100
Singer, Peter, 5
Spina bifida, 71
Steptoe, Dr Patrick, 27
Sterilisation, 44, 91 et seq., 104
Suicide, 55, 57
Surrogate Motherhood, 27-8, 36-9, 120 et seq.

Tay-Sachs disease, 25
Therapeutic Donor Insemination (see 'artificial insemination')
Tooley, Michael, 5

Warnock Committee, 81, 128
Welfare principle, 12, 16, 17
Wrongful life claims, 29, 103

Table of Cases

A v C, p.121
Adoption Application 212/86, p.127 n.16
Akron v Akron Center for Reproductive Health, p.59 n.2
Allaire v St. Luke's Hospital, p.100 n.7

Baby M, pp.28, 35, 37 and 126
Baby X, p.101 n.14
Baird v Attorney General, p.59 n.3
Barber v Superior Court, p.59 n.6
Berman v Allan, p.103 n.20
Bonbrest v Kotz, p.100 n.8
Bonner v Moran, p.59 n.5
Bowen v American Hospital Association, p.71 n.33

C v S, p.15; p.59 n.1
Canterbury v Spence, p.69 n.26
Carey v Population Services International, p.14
Childrens' Aid Society and Unborn Child of L.T. and G.K., p.113 n.41
Cleveland Board of Education v LaFleur, p.104 n.27
Cobbs v Grant, p.60 n.8 and n.9; p.62 n.12
Commonwealth v Cass, p.101 n.11
Conservatorship of Drabick, p.65 n.15
Conservatorship of Morrison, p.65 n.15
Conservatorship of Waltz, p.69 n.27
Cruzan v Harmon, p.66 n.21; p.68 n.23
Curlender v Bio-Science Laboratories, pp.103, 104

Davis v Davis, pp.33, 35 and 36
Dietrich v Inhabitants of Northampton, p.100 n.1 and n.7
Docherty v McGlynn, p.95 n.60
Drobner v Peters, p.100 n.7

Elliot v Joicey, p.107 n.35
Emeh v Kensington Area Health Authority, p.104 n.24
Erickson v Dilgard, p.66 n.19

Finlayson, p.113, n.44
F. v West Berkshire Health Authority, p.16 n.20; pp.94, 95 and 96

Gallacher v Duke Hospital, p.104 n.23
Gildiner v Thomas Jefferson University Hospital, p.103 n.21
Gillick v West Norfolk and Wisbech Area Health Authority, pp.8, 13, 14; p.59 n.2; p.59 n.3; p.69 n.26; pp.84, 85, 86, 87, 88, 89, 90
Gleitman v Cosgrave, p.103 n.18
Gold v Haringey Area Health Authority, p.104 n.24
Grodin v Grodin, p.115
Guardianship of Eberhandy, p.67 n.22
Guardianship of Grant, p.60 n.7
Guardianship of Phillip B. p.74 n.44

Hall v State, p.73 n.41
Harbeson v Parke-Davis, p.104 n.23
Harvey v Harvey, p.87
Hewer v Bryant, p.87 n.21 and n.23
H. M. A. v Semple, p.82 n.4

Table of Cases

Hollis v Commonwealth of Kentucky, p.101 n.9

Jefferson v Griffin Spalding County Hospital Authority, p.113
J. F. K. Memorial Hospital v Bludsworth, p.70 n.13; p.76 n.54; p.100 n.43
Joswick v Lenox Hill Hospital, p.74 n.47
J. V. v State, p.75 n.41

Lane v Candura, p.70 n.30
Leadbetter v N. C. B., p.108 n.36
Lydia E. v Hall Hospital, p.70 n.28

McCluskey v H. M. A., p.101 n.10
McConnell v Beverly Enterprises – Connecticut Inc., p.66 n.20
McKay v Essex Health Authority, p.104 n.25; p.123 n.11
Magnolia Coca Cola Bottling Co. v Jordan, p.101 n.7
Matter of Sackenwicz, p.70 n.29
Matter of Spring, p.70 n.28
Montreal Tramways v Leveille, p.100 n.2

Pamela Rae Stewart, p.116
Parpalaix Case, p.34
Paton v British Pregnancy Advisory Services, p.15; p.59 n.1
People v Robbins, p.65 n.17
Pet. of Nemser, p.64 n.14
Pierce v Society of Sisters, p.73 n.40
Planned Parenthood of Missouri v Danforth, p.14; p.59 n.1
Prince v Massachusetts, p.73 n.40 and n.42

Raleigh Fitkin-Paul Memorial Hospital v Anderson, p.113 n.45
Rasmussen v Fleming, p.64 n.13
R v Arthur, p.11
R v Gyngall, p.94 n.54
R v Smith, p.60 n.9

R v Tait, p.101 n.12
Re A. C., p.114
Re Adoption Application (Payment for Adoption), p.27 n.15
Re B (1973), p.74 n.51
Re B (1981), p.11
Re B (1987), pp.94, 95, 96, 97
Re Barry, p.76 n.56
Re Cicero, p.113 n.44
Re D (a Minor), pp.92, 94
Re D (a Minor) v Berkshire County Council, p.101 n.14
Re Dittrick Infant, p.112 n.40
Re Richner, p.60 n.10
Re Eric B., p.73 n.41
Re Eve, pp.93, 94
Re F, p.101 n.14
Re F (in utero), p.112 n.39
Re Grady, p.66 n.21; p.67 n.22
Re Green, p.74 n.48
Re Guardianship of Browning, p.60 n.8; p.68 n.24
Re Heir, p.60 n.8
Re Hofbauer, p.73 n.43
Re Hudson, p.74 n.49
Re Jobes, p.76 n.55
Re Maydun, p.114, n.48
Re P (a Minor), p.15
Re Phillip B., p.12; p.74 n.44; p.113 n.44
Re Seiferth, p.74 n.50
Re W., p.74 n.53
Re Westchester County Medical Center (O'Connor), p.66 n.20; p.68 n.23
Reyes v Superior Court, p.116
Roe v Wade, p.105 n.30
Royal College of Nursing v DHSS, p.84 n.11

Salgo v Leland Stanford Jr. University Board of Trustees, p.62 n.12
Schloendorff v Society of New York Hospitals, p.65 n.16
S. v Distillers and Co. (Biochemicals) Ltd., p.102 n.16

Table of Cases

Sidaway v Bethlem Royal Hospital and Others, p.65 n.16
Smith v Aukland Hospital Board, p.65 n.16
Smith v Brennan, p.100 n.8
Smith v Jones, p.38 n.37
Speck v Finnegold, p.103 n.19
Stallman v Youngquist, p.115
Strunk v Strunk, p.91 n.43
Superintendant of Belchertown State School v Sailewicz, p.91 n.42

Taft v Taft, p.114 n.49
Thake v Maurice, p.104 n.24
T. v T., p.94 n.55
Turpin v Sortini, p.104 n.23

Udale v Bloomsbury Area Health Authority, p.104 n.24
U. S. v University Hospital, p.74 n.46

Walker v Great Northern Railway Co. of Ireland, p.100 n.1
Weber v Stony Brook Hospital, p.70 n.31; p.74 n.45
Wentzel v Montgomery General Hospital, p.74 n.52
Whitehall v Whitehall, p.113 n.43

York v Jones, p.33 n.23 and n.25
Young v Oakland General Hospital, p.64 n.13 and n.14